Bristol Radical Par

Angela Carter's 'Provincial Bohemia'

The counterculture in 1960s and 1970s Bristol and Bath

Stephen E. Hunt

ISBN 978-1-911522-52-2

Bristol Radical History Group. 2020.
www.brh.org.uk
brh@brh.org.uk

Contents

Acknowledgements

All of the following in some way helped to make this research happen and to bring some of the hidden history of the West Country's counterculture to light. Several knew Angela Carter in person. I'm immensely grateful for their memories, insights, help with production, rummaging in archives and other contributions.

Ian A. Anderson, Bob Baker, Peter Bild, Eugene Byrne, Shirley Cameron, Nick Curry, Glyn Davies, Sarah Davies, Mary Flitton, Bob Gale, Nick Gilbert, 'Rustic' Rod Goodway, Dennis Gould, Nick Gray, Rich Grove, Gary Hicks, Trevor Houghton, Richard Jones, Dave Lawton, Peter M. Le Mare, Roland Miller, Christine Molan, Richard Musgrove, Ed Newsom, Phil Owen, Al Read (c1942-2019), John Row, Fiona Scott, Helene Scott, Barbara Segal, Will Simpson, Rod Stradling, Gordon Strong, Dave Thorne, Pat Thorne and Heathcote Williams (1941-2017). The teams at the University of Bristol Special Collections (Ian Coates, Michael Richardson and Hannah Lowery), Bristol Reference Library (Dawn Dyer and colleagues), Malcolm Boyns and colleagues at Bristol Archives and the British Library who helped me to source primary materials.

Waiter, waiter
There's a fly in my soup!
Yes, madame,
It's trouser soup!

(courtesy of Neil Curry)

Introduction

There's no denying that towards the end of the decade everyday life, even where I was living, in Bristol, took on the air of a continuous improvisation... the particularly leafy and graceful bit of Bristol where I lived attracted festal behaviour. Carpe diem. *Pleasure. It didn't have to cost much, either.*[1]

Angela Carter (1940-1992) did not name Bristol or Bath in any of her novels. Nevertheless, while these place-names were written out of her writing, her early writing was written out of her experience of place. The purpose of this booklet is two-fold. First, its intention is to take Angela Carter's location in 1960s Clifton, Bristol and 1970s Walcot, Bath as a point of departure to explore the broader artistic, radical and experimental communities that flourished in those years. Second, it is to discover and reveal some non-literary influences during her formative years as a writer in the West Country. The novelist's standing as a rising literary star happened within and alongside the sun- and moon-shaped architecture of these upmarket Georgian and Regency districts, once the home to a bohemian counterculture, now substantially re-gentrified. Often, the regional counterculture has been overlooked, while attention has focused upon the 'underground' as a phenomenon confined to the capital. A stroll through this cultural and geographic territory is, therefore, an opportunity to explore something of the under-researched 'provincial' 1960s and 1970s alternative society.

In a sense, Angela Carter's residence in Bristol and Bath was incidental to her ambition as a writer. She wasn't born in the West Country, and she could have as well lived anywhere else. Indeed, she did. London. Tokyo. Providence, Rhode Island. Adelaide. Sheffield and Norwich. Furthermore, as her friend Christopher Frayling hints, to be called a regional 'novelist based in the West Country'[2] was to be labelled in a faintly condescending way, that suggested a parochial worldview, despite the company of such acclaimed literary forebears as Tobias Smollett, Fanny Burney, Jane Austen, Mary Shelley, Thomas Hardy, Richard Jefferies, John Cowper Powys and Sylvia Townsend Warner. In any case, as Zoe Brennan points out, Carter brought something of an outsider's perspective, perhaps a London-centric view, to the West Country.[3] Yet, I will

1 Angela Carter, 'Truly, It Felt Like Year One', 209-216 in *Very Heaven: Looking Back at the 1960s*, ed. by Sarah Maitland (London: Virago, 1988), 212.
2 Christopher Frayling, *Inside the Bloody Chamber: On Angela Carter, The Gothic and Other Weird Tales* (London: Oberon Books, 2015), 17.
3 Zoe Brennan, 'Angela Carter's "Bristol Trilogy": A Gothic Perspective on Bristol's 1960s Counterculture', 162-182 in *Literary Bristol: Writers and the City*, ed. by Marie Mulvey-Roberts (Bristol: Redcliffe Press / Regional History Centre, University of the West of England, 2015), 179.

argue that in Carter's case the experience of living in Bristol and Bath during the 1960s and 1970s was the source of many transformative influences in the making of one of the late twentieth-century's most distinctive novelists. The beauty and forcefulness of her writing is a confluence of an intense imagination, watered by an eclectic love of literature, a politically informed drive to dismantle injustice and curiosity about everything. It was especially during the years when she and her husband, Paul Carter, lived in Royal York Crescent, Clifton (1961-1969) that she developed her identity and found her writerly voice. When Carter lived in Bath (1973-1975), mostly living at 5 Hay Hill, she moved towards the height of her creative powers, working on themes expressed in short stories such as those in *Fireworks* (1974) and bearing ghastly fruit in *The Bloody Chamber* (1979).

I hesitated to write this pamphlet. There is surely little to add to the discussion of the life, works and ideas of such a revered and well-loved author. Yet Angela Carter's links to the West Country have received limited attention. 2016 was a watershed year in addressing this gap. It was the year of publication of Edmund Gordon's extensive biography, *The Invention of Angela Carter*, detailing the circumstances of the composition of Carter's first novels, together forming what has become known as the 'Bristol trilogy'. December 2016 also saw the launch of the artistic and biographical exhibition entitled 'Strange Worlds: The Vision of Angela Carter', held at the Royal West of England Academy in Whiteladies Road, Bristol, which ran until March 2017. A major new documentary, *Angela Carter: Of Wolves and Women,* featuring interviews with Carter's close friend in Bristol and later illustrator, Corrina Sargood, and fellow novelists Anne Enright, Margaret Atwood, Salman Rushdie and Jeanette Winterson, was screened on BBC2 in August 2018. Director Emma Rice's adaptation of Carter's final novel, *Wise Children*, was staged to critical acclaim at the Bristol Old Vic from January to February 2019. However, while Brixton boasts a street named 'Angela Carter Close', there is still no visible tribute in Bristol or Bath. Despite recent attention to the novelist's residence in Bristol and Bath, her relationship to the cities' countercultures has been little explored, not just in terms of their influence but as deserving of attention in their own right.

There is more to add concerning the ways that Bristol and Bath feature in Angela Carter's journey as a writer and commentator. *Angela Carter: Of Wolves and Women* controversially frames her decade in Bristol as a time when she stayed at home as a lonely housewife, writing novels compulsively as a refuge from her disappointing and claustrophobic marriage to Paul Carter. The suggestion that she 'escaped into circles ever more bohemian' in flight from her marriage is perhaps only partially true. While she was certainly

Ground Floor Flat, 38 Royal York Crescent. The Carters' address 1962-69.

intrigued by the bohemian life that she discovered, and was embraced by the Clifton bohemians, husband Paul Carter was also fully part of this social scene. Salman Rushdie observed that 'Angela's engagement with Japan [1969-1971], I think, made her who she was'.[4] Again this is not untrue, but it is far from the whole truth. Alternative style and writerly confidence were already integral to her presentation of self during the 1960s. In 1988, Angela Carter referred to the 'festal behaviour' that had reigned in her area of Bristol two decades before, which she experienced first-hand. Gary Hicks knew her in his role as one-time editor of the University of Bristol student publication, *Nonesuch* magazine, in which capacity he published some of her early essays while she was in her twenties. He remembered her carefully cultivated appearance at that time during the mid-1960s, writing that Angela 'used to adopt a Paris left bank persona, as I recall, beret, corduroy jeans, Gauloises cigarettes etc'.[5] By the time she left Bristol, she was an established author, as the BBC2 documentary notes, having written five novels and a substantial number of published essays and poems during her formative years in the city.

4 Salman Rushdie interview, *Angela Carter: Of Wolves and Women,* directed by Jude Ho (Broadcast BBC, 4 August 2018).
5 Gary Hicks, e-mail to the author (4 January 2019).

Many others partook of the creative and festal spirit. It has been with their memories, stories and insights that I have tried to create a picture of the counterculture that emerged in the early 1960s and was in full swing by the 1970s. The first thing to acknowledge about the counterculture is that it is a shape-shifting thing and one difficult to define. Theodore Roszak is variously credited with or accused of having coined the term 'counterculture', which he defined as youthful opposition to 'technocracy'. In *The Making of a Counter Culture*, he hesitantly affirmed that there was a 'spirit of the times' that demanded recognition and hoped that some kind of solid phenomenon still existed even after he had allowed exceptions 'to slip through the sieve of one's generalizations'.[6] The literary historian Patricia Waugh speaks of the 'extreme countercultural abandonment of rationality' rooted in Romanticism.[7] A form of anti-capitalism, Romanticism could be anti-rationalist but its best manifestations were warmly rational, concerned as they were with connectivity and vitally opposed to alienation, rather than aesthetic concerns running untethered. So, the nature of the counterculture and the value of the term are uncertain and contested.

I am offering a wide definition of the counterculture, considering it as embracing a thoroughgoing critique of social structures underpinned by hierarchy, capitalism and the state and manifestations of anti-militarism and internationalism, class struggle, educational reform, women's and gay liberation, alternative media, experimentation in the creative arts, rising ecological awareness, psychedelia, an interest in non-Western cultural forms and practices, housing activism, squatting and communal living, festivity and other manifestations of dissent. Politically, underpinning this diverse number of concerns, collectively expressed in the New Social Movements, the emergence of the New Left sought to reclaim and reinvigorate socialist traditions discredited by the manifest failure of Soviet and Eastern European states to replace capitalism with just, equitable and sustainable alternatives. Much of the Sixties bohemianism and counterculture falls within the categories of Romantic anti-capitalism that Robert Sayre and Michael Löwy set out, defining analytical categories from fascistic elements (perhaps most notoriously exemplified during the 1960s by the Manson Family), to forms of Libertarian Romanticism (represented during the 1960s, for instance by Situationists or the social ecologist ideas of Murray Bookchin). It is important that Sayre and Löwy affirm that:

6 Theodore Roszak, *The Making of a Counter Culture: Reflections on the Technocratic Society and its Youthful Opposition* (Garden City, NY: Anchor Books, 1969), xiii.
7 Patricia Waugh, *Harvest of the Sixties: English Literature and its Background 1960 to 1990* (Oxford: Oxford University Press, 1995), 121.

Romanticism represents a deep-seated revolt against [the bourgeois class] and the society it rules. If Romanticism is in its essence anti-capitalist, it is the antithesis of a bourgeois ideology.[8]

During the 1960s and 1970s this revolt took the form, to use Timothy Leary's famous terms, of both 'dropping out and tuning in, of both escapism and the energetic pursuit of alternatives. To keep the argument on track in the local context, I will look at an article published in the University of Bristol's *Nonesuch News* in 1971, which airs the contrasting perspectives of a Conservative, a commentator who attempts to represent the counterculture and a revolutionary socialist. The political legacy of the 1960s and 1970s counterculture is uncertain in so far as the contested ideas that emerged at that time are still being fought out with unknown outcomes. 'The personal is political' became a key slogan and progress on cultural matters was achieved. Nevertheless, the struggle to undertake a social revolution, able to achieve a more equitable distribution of wealth and power, and to implement participatory democratically in all areas of life have stalled, while aspirations to achieve a transition to environmental sustainability have also not been met. Indeed, the inspiration for the counterculture must be set against the enduring social conservatism of mainstream culture, documented in *White Heat*, historian Dominic Sandbrook's account of Britain in the 'Swinging Sixties'.[9]

Many of the people that Angela Carter mixed with socially in Bristol, and that inhabit her early novels, shared in a bohemian counterculture, meaning that in significant areas of their lives they challenged or existed outside of the norms and values of mainstream society. During the 1960s and 1970s alternative lifestyle could be expressed through some or all of the following: a livelihood sustained outside of the wage system either by self-employment, living as a student, artisanship or the black economy, radical approaches to housing, education and medicine, participation in sub-cultures defined and identified by music, dress codes and design, left-libertarian perspectives which adopted direct democracy in the workplace and community and direct action in preference to conventional party politics, experimentation in altered states of consciousness (through drugs or spiritual practices), cohabitation in preference to marriage and questioning of traditional relationships, rejection of monotheistic religion, promoting sustainability and perhaps above all, living according to some intrinsic ethos and motivation whether creative, spiritual, political or hedonistic.

8 Robert Sayre and Michael Löwy, 'Figures of Romantic Anti-Capitalism' 88.
9 Dominic Sandbrook, *White Heat: A History of Britain in the Swinging Sixties* (London: Abacus, 2007), esp. Chapter 10.

Since such a counterculture is fluid and diverse in its preoccupations, I have carried out a wide-ranging survey of people, some who knew Angela Carter personally, and some who lived in the same areas of Bristol and Bath, especially during what is sometimes described as the 'Long Sixties', from the Beatnik days of the late 1950s to the pre-Thatcherite years of the mid-1970s. As a consequence, I have undertaken to test, demonstrate and reflect upon the value of oral history and other primary sources in bringing into focus the blurred edges of literary history. Such an approach at once exploits serendipity, yet inevitably causes the researcher to confront disappointing obstacles, as memories fade and those able to share first-hand experiences of the period concerned pass away. The kind of history from below approach,[10] valued by grassroots seekers of hidden histories such as Bristol Radical History Group, thrives on such direct accounts and recognises their urgency. An obituary for the poet, John James, for example, who studied at the University of Bristol and was a part of the Clifton community during the 1960s, appeared in May 2018. Furthermore, archives and documents are in peril. The Bath Labour Party headquarters, based in Pierrepont Street for decades, relocated in 2017, with abundant papers apparently disposed of as the premises downsized from four storeys to a small office in Walcot Street. Disappointingly, therefore, minutes and other records of Angela Carter's active involvement as Secretary of the Labour Party for the Bathwick ward during the mid-1970s may have been lost recently.

Carter was never a narrowly didactic writer but always a political author. The Campaign for Nuclear Disarmament was a cause célèbre and shared concern for Angela and Paul Carter when they first met during the late 1950s. The heavily politicised world of the folk revival provided the soundtrack for the anti-nuclear movement, so helped her to find and develop her voice both as a folk musician and an astute commentator on current affairs. In subsequent years the peace movement was also to overlap closely with the women's movement and the New Left; the concerns of all three became significant influences on Angela's Carter's outlook. The early chapters, therefore, concertina out Carter's participation in the overlapping politics of the CND and folk scenes, and discuss their influence on her work.

Upon moving to Clifton, Angela Carter found the convivial local folk clubs to be an early stimulus for ideas and inspiration. In Bristol, she broke out of initial feelings of social isolation to immerse herself in such overlapping

10 Historical approach first associated with the *History Workshop Journal* and now apparent in many 'people's histories'. A recommended account of the issues involved is Anthony Iles and Tom Roberts, *All Knees and Elbows of Susceptibility and Refusal: Reading History from Below* (London: Mute / Strickland Distribution / Transmission Gallery, 2012).

and divergent milieux as local pubs, the University of Bristol, Bristol Zoo and the burgeoning counterculture of what she termed 'provincial Bohemia'.[11] No expression of genius is spontaneous and transcendent; for Angela Carter, it was the world of folk music, initially introduced by husband Paul that helped her to flourish socially and was an enduring source for the characterisation, variety, colour and narrative approach that nurtured her phenomenal literary imagination. The biographical outlines of this story are known through Gordon's *Invention of Angela Carter*, along with accounts of friends and earlier critics. However, untold elements of the truth still rival fiction for strangeness. She wrote extraordinary stories because she read widely and adventurously, mixed with extraordinary people and did extraordinary things.

Three of Carter's earliest novels were written in and about Bristol and have since been grouped as the 'Bristol trilogy': *Shadow Dance* (1966), *Several Perceptions* (1968) and *Love* (1971). While Bristol is unnamed, the city and particularly the then bohemian circles of Clifton form the context for these texts. A psychogeographical stroll around Clifton and the immediately surrounding districts of Hotwells, Cliftonwood, Cotham, Stoke Bishop and Redland helps to picture the habitat in which her characters lived. The alternative society that she experienced (and with it the festal behaviour) have long since disappeared almost entirely from the area, to some extent resurfacing in other forms, in other times and in other places. Nevertheless, bombed fewer times during the Blitz and re-developed to a lesser extent than other areas of Bristol, the district retains much historical and cultural interest and has still many tales to tell.[12] Some of this legacy relates to the revelation of vast profits from the slave trade and tobacco industry behind the gorgeous and genteel facades of Clifton's impressive architecture. But radical and dissident traditions had also emerged in the area by the eighteenth and nineteenth centuries. Here, Thomas Beddoes and Humphry Davy conducted their famous medical experiments using laughing gas at the Pneumatic Institute, portrait artists Ellen and Rolinda Sharples excelled at their art, the aunt and

---

11 Quoted from Angela Carter interview with John Haffenden (1984) by Marc O'Day, '"Mutability is Having a Field Day": The Sixties Aura of Angela Carter's Bristol Trilogy,' pp. 24-58 in *Flesh and the Mirror: Essays and the Art of Angela Carter*. Ed. by Lorna Sage (London: Virago, 1994), 24.

12 Bristol City Council have produced a detailed survey of Clifton's designated conservation area, which is described as 'of "outstanding interest" and considered to be of national significance' (4): City Design Group, Bristol City Council, *Conservation Area 5 Clifton & Hotwells: Character Appraisal and Management Proposals* (Bristol: Bristol City Council, 2010): http://www.cliftonhotwells.org.uk/resources/clifton-and-hotwells-character-appraisal.pdf [accessed 28 November 2018]. The conservation report also notes that 'Clifton & Hotwells is abutted on all sides by neighbouring conservation areas' (2).

niece partnership Edith Cooper and Katherine Bradley forged the persona of 'Michael Field' to co-author their poetry and plays, while the literary critic and gay historian John Addington Symonds, who described himself as 'a born Bohemian',[13] lived at Clifton Hill House.

Clifton has been widely derided elsewhere in the city as the seat of class privilege, both due to its historic role in the periods of slavery and empire, and in present times as the home and playground of the rich. Indeed, the slogan 'Don't Bomb Baghdad, Bomb Clifton!' appeared on Church Road, Redfield at the outbreak of the Iraq War in 2003! Harsh neo-liberalism and the imposition of austerity as a matter of policy in recent years has seen something of a throwback to the sharp class divides of the era in which the area was constructed. The district now boasts the most expensive housing in the city, with gated mansions at Leigh Woods and properties around the Downs being the preserve of multi-millionaires, and Clifton Village popularly associated with affluence and the elite culture of expensive restaurants and wine bars, exclusive clubs and upmarket shops. While some parts of Clifton remained 'posh', however, others were far less prosperous during the 1960s than they had been before the Second World War. Writer and musician Gordon Strong described the area as it first experienced it when he moved to the city as a student in 1966:

> You see the thing about Clifton was that it wasn't a place to live. I mean it was a very isolated little community which had kind of frozen in the '50s. It didn't cope very well with the '60s because people had got these huge houses, for instance, and they were becoming a liability.[14]

Such a situation made for affordable housing, creating opportunities for the creative, disaffected and dissident people that made up the counterculture. During the 1970s, however, housing activists such as the Clifton Tenants' Association, squatters and alternative media publications were already campaigning against the combined impact of market forces and shifting council policy, socially reconfiguring the area as they forced up prices.[15] By

13 In a letter to Henry Graham Dakyns, 19 July 1890), according to Rictor Norton, *The Life of John Addington Symonds* (1997) [online] [Accessed 30 July 2018].
14 Gordon Strong, interview with the author (La Ruca Café, Gloucester Road, Bristol 28 February 2019).
15 As we shall see, locally, the Clifton Tenants' Association was formed in the early 1970s to campaign for affordable housing provision and tenants' rights against profiteering landlords. In 2018 local estate agents Ocean describe the Clifton area as 'one of the oldest, most affluent and most beautiful parts of the city', with 'some of Bristol's most expensive property': https://www.oceanhome.co.uk/location_guides/clifton [accessed 28 November 2018].

the 1980s and 1990s, therefore, the area had become contested territory, a front-line against gentrification with similarities to the way that the dissident street cultures such as those in Bristol's city centre locations Stokes Croft and the Bear Pit are controversially experiencing social cleansing in the present day.

It is helpful to recreate a sense of this former alternative Clifton, now largely on the fringes of the area, for two reasons. First, to understand the spirit and context of Carter's formative writings. Second, and more importantly, an acquaintance with the countercultural aspects of the district help to understand the dynamics of the shifting human geography of Bristol as a city, embroiled in multiple class and cultural conflicts relating to its complex and contested legacies. Carter began her degree in the English Department of the University of Bristol in 1962, graduating in 1965. The University contributed to the cultural buzz in the surrounding area. Carter also took great inspiration from the community she saw and experienced and in which she embedded herself. The fortunes of formerly affluent Clifton and Hotwells were impacted by the Second World War, and affected by demographic shifts, such as the decline of the large families of the Victorian and Edwardian eras with their supporting domestic servants. This had a social-economic impact since, consequently, the large houses were divided into more affordable residential units. Dwelling in the vast multi-occupancy complex of a Regency crescent, Carter tapped into, and added to, the stored goodness of the hive mind of Clifton bohemia, which was to feed creative endeavours in the city for years to come.

Nonetheless, 1960s Bristol was no utopia and Carter does not portray it as such. Jane Jacobs, the famous American commentator on urban space, was a great champion of planning arrangements that nurtured diverse and cohesive communities, yet was nuanced in her approach, expressing scepticism about the way in which 'Neighbourhood is a word that has begun to sound like a valentine'.[16] Speaking of neighbourhoods nearer to home in Bristol, the late Jeremy Brent, in his study of Southmead, spoke of community as 'a combination of thoughts, dreams, actions and materiality',[17] yet was aware that these could equate to curses, nightmares, abuse and endemic poverty and shared recognition with Jacobs that, however desirable, community development was not something that could be readily engineered by external agencies. Carter would have been aware of economic tensions in the districts in which she lived. Capitalism divides, exploits and expands regardless of the systemic problems it generates, such as social dysfunction linked to alienation

---

16 Jane Jacobs, *The Death and Life of Great American Cities: The Failure of Town Planning* [1961] (London: Penguin, 1965), 122.

17 Jeremy Brent, *Searching for Community: Representation, Power and Action on an Urban Estate* (Bristol: Policy Press, 2009), 228

and extensive inequalities in wealth and power, born out for instance by the street violence and evictions that take place in *Shadow Dance* and the depression and deprivation that appear in *Several Perceptions* and *Love*. At the same time, Carter celebrated the opportunities and the increasing social diversity that the collapse of Empire had brought about, since change and possibility also unleashed a utopian potential. Some of the jottings in her journal capture a sense of a city and society in transition. The following snapshots, written by Carter in 1966, describe developments in Bristol's Lawrence Hill area:

Round here, they are pulling the houses down & building flats. Towers of light in the black night sky. Rubble beside the road. Empty shops, their windows boarded up. […]

I went up Lawrence Hill. It was a smoked gold day, quite warm. The towers look nice in the sun, surrounded by their smooth lawns. The houses being pulled down, little terraces, & gutted shops with a side gone, ripped off; patchwork of exposed walls in muted colours; one former café had a hole in the back wall so you could see right through it to the towers beyond.

An archetypal old man stood on a corner, which he must have known formerly; his large Andy Capp was checked & buttoned down, his trousers braced high around the base of his ribs.

W. Love, tobacconist; boarded up & soon to be demolished. At the end of a boarded up terrace, a corner shop, Williams, corsetiere, with incredible [illegible] looking corsets in the window, bright pink & laced up the front like the first act of 'Giselle'. A second hand clothes shop, with second hand paperbacks & magazines in the window. And this seaside feeling because at the end of the street was nothing but a range of sunlit distance, nothing left anymore. A pub, still open.[18]

Evaluative language is largely absent from Carter's descriptions and her attitude towards the developments is mixed. She described the appearance of blocks as looking 'nice in the sun' by day and like 'towers of light' by night. At the same time there are hints of nostalgia in her portrayal of the loss of more traditional terraces and the amenities and characters that went with them, due to 'slum' clearance. The observations above record processes reminiscent of those that sociologists Peter Willmott and Michael Young

18 British Library Archive: Angela Carter Papers: Journal Add MS 88899/1/91:1966-1968.

analysed in their famous study *Family and Kinship in East London* (1957). With the benefit of hindsight, and a degree of posthumous irony, we know that, 50 years later, Lawrence Hill is one of Bristol's most deprived locations, with a finding that 36% of the ward's residents were deemed to be 'income deprived', according to a Bristol City Council report, based on a survey undertaken in 2015.[19]

Carter's years in Bristol coincided not only with profound social and cultural change, therefore, but with an immense and controversial re-engineering of the city's physical infrastructure, in which processes that radically reconfigured the built environment were accompanied by a significant impact upon the natural environment. During the late 1960s and early 1970s, several groups appeared which aimed to protect and enhance Bristol's architectural heritage, together with the many green spaces that remained within the city and the countryside beyond. By 1972, for example, the newly-established Bristol Friends of the Earth group, had found common ground with civic conservation groups, joining forces to oppose the Bristol Development Plan.[20] The three strands of the city's ecology movement—lobbying and information campaigns, green initiatives and ecological direct action against the worst excesses of environmental destruction—were to contribute to Bristol's reputation as an environmentally-aware city in the decades to come.

Such campaigns to fight for Bristol's physical and community integrity are closely connected to another thread of interest in what follows, being the strong cultural identity that is found in and around the city. This is expressed in the widespread celebration of Bristol as a city of migration, with the diverse traditions and creative mixes it has embraced. As we shall see, since there is a perception that funding is London-centric, with the capital attracting more funding than provincial areas, Bristol has developed a powerful ethos of Do-It-Yourself culture. This has been productive of countless home-grown cultural initiatives and creative collaborations that were already underway during the 1960s and 1970s. Furthermore, while many creative artists and

19 Bristol City Council, *Deprivation in Bristol 2015: The Mapping of Deprivation within Bristol Local Authority Area* [online] (Bristol: Bristol City Council, 2015), 2: https://www.bristol. gov.uk/documents/20182/32951/Deprivation+in+Bristol+2015/429b2004-eeff-44c5-8044-9e7dcd002faf [accessed 4 August 2018]. The proportion of income-deprived people in Clifton in 2015 was estimated at 5%.

20 Brownlee, *Bristol's Green Roots*, 42. According to Richard Bland, the Bristol Ecology Party held its first meeting in a pub on Blackboy Hill, Clifton in 1976; see Clifton and Hotwells Improvement Society website. Richard Bland, 'The Green Side of Bristol 8 in the Context of Forty Years of Environmental Change', Forty Years of CHIS, 1968–2008: http://www. cliftonhotwells.org.uk/newsletters?newsletterdate=2008-01 [accessed 7 October 2018].6.

political activists aspired to move to London, the 'provincial bohemia' that Angela Carter cherished was also sustained. At around 120 miles from central London, Bristol was far away enough not to be in the shadow of the much larger city, especially before the construction of the M4 from the mid-1960s to the early 1970s. At the same time, it was sufficiently connected not to be isolated or to suffer the insularity that can beset smaller, less well-connected centres of population. Many in the counterculture, for instance, would regularly hitchhike to the capital. It may be that Bristol maintained its cultural vitality because its location is something of a 'Goldilocks' zone in relation to the metropolis.

As I have suggested, *Angela Carter: Of Wolves and Women,* acknowledges that the novelist's years in Bristol were astonishingly productive. Yet the representation (perhaps partly self-invented) of her life in Clifton as a repressed and reclusive housewife spending her hours indoors typing frantically between endless domestic chores is incomplete and misleading. As her journals demonstrate and contemporaries testify, she liked to go out and either socialise or simply observe the street life and pub life in all parts of Bristol. As the second largest city in the south of England, after London,[21] Bristol was, and remains, a hotbed of activism, able to sustain Carter's development as a politically engaged and committed commentator throughout the Cold War. Much of the detail of this colourful world has been revealed during the course of my current research. Intriguingly, memoirs by both Susannah Clapp and Christopher Frayling recorded that their friend had cited the anarchists she socialised with in Bristol as major influences on her ideas, alongside her hugely varied literary inspirations.[22] Who were the Bristol anarchists? How was Carter connected to the anarchic performance and happenings in Bristol and Bath's far-out fringes? And who were the Bristol Dwarfs that hailed from the basement of the home of her one-time lover John Orsborn?

Few critics have paid much attention to the importance of locality or the counterculture to her life and work in Bristol and Bath. My intention

21 Bristol's population was just under 425,000 in 1961, rising to approximately 428,000 in 1971, before decreasing significantly by the time of the first census in the new millennium to around 380,000. Source: GB Historical GIS / University of Portsmouth, Bristol City/UA [Unitary Authority] through time: Population Statistics: Total Population, *A Vision of Britain through Time*: http://www.visionofbritain.org.uk/unit/10056676/cube/TOT_POP (15 November 2016) [accessed via Wayback machine 28 November 2018]. Bristol's population has since increased sharply again to its current estimate which is 459, 300 and continuing to rise. Source: Bristol City Council, *The Population of Bristol* (November 2018): https://www.bristol.gov.uk/statistics-census-information/the-population-of-bristol [accessed 28 November 2018].
22 Susannah Clapp, *A Card from Angela Carter* (London: Bloomsbury, 2012), 51; Christopher Frayling, *Inside the Bloody Chamber: Angela Carter, the Gothic and Other Weird Tales* (London: Oberon Books, 2015), 37.

Booming Bristol' image from the *Evening Post* (10 March 1967).

in what follows, therefore, is to foreground what is, tantalisingly, for the most part just mentioned in passing in much academic literary criticism. Carter's friend Lorna Sage, for example, refers to Joseph's situation in *Several Perceptions,* mentioning 'a shiftless world in which hippies and vagrants, tramps and a whore [...] form a drifting counter-culture'.[23] Linden Peach speaks briefly of the Bristol trilogy's 'imaginative response to provincial bohemian life as it happened at the time in bedsits, flats, cafes and coffee bars where somehow the boundaries between art and life became blurred.'[24] Sarah Gamble dwelled longer on the way that Carter 'wrote of the countercultural environment' and commented astutely that the topic was attractive to her 'because it represents a strategy by which she could negotiate the boundaries between fantasy and concrete political action'.[25] Two valuable essays, Marc O'Day's '"Mutability is Having a Field Day"'(1994) and Zoe Brennan's more recent 'Angela Carter's "Bristol Trilogy"' (2015) start to explore the significance of the counterculture in the West Country, where the novelist was to live for half of her adult life.

Angela Carter once wrote: 'I was a wide-eyed provincial beatnik and there were a lot of them around'.[26] What follows pivots around Angela Carter's life and work in the 1960s and early 1970s, stepping out from Royal York Crescent and Hay Hill into the circles of the beatniks and bohemians of which she speaks. There were, indeed, a lot of them around.

23 Lorna Sage, *Angela Carter*, Writers and their work series (Plymouth: Northcote House, 1994), 16-17.
24 Linden Peach, *Angela Carter*, Macmillan Modern Novelists series (Basingstoke: Macmillan, 1998), 26-27.
25 Sarah Gamble, *Angela Carter: Writing from the Front Line* (Edinburgh: Edinburgh University Press, 1997), 43.
26 Quoted in Lorna Sage, 'The Savage Sideshow: A Profile of Angela Carter,' *New Review* 4.39/40 (1977), 54.

'Exhibitions of mass sanity':
Angela Carter and the Campaign for Nuclear Disarmament

> [CND] *aroused the interest and enthusiasm of a whole generation*
> *of young people, giving them not only a base for political activity but*
> *also a forum for all kinds of fresh ideas. It widened the horizons of the*
> *young in a way probably unprecedented in British history. This was*
> *the generation that, largely through CND, became the foundation for*
> *virtually all radical movements in the next ten to twenty years.*[27]

Angela and Paul Carter were among the activists who supported the Campaign for Nuclear Disarmament (CND) during its early years. CND was founded in London at a mass public meeting at Westminster's Central Hall in February 1958. It was, in part, CND that brought Angela and Paul together as a couple. Angela later suggested that she married Paul because 'I finally bumped into somebody who would go to Godard movies with me and on CND marches and even have sexual intercourse with me, although he insisted we should be engaged first.'[28] This implies that CND marches were already underway when they first met, so they did not attend the first march to Aldermaston (Atomic Weapons Establishment) as a couple in 1958, nor perhaps the Easter 1959 march, since Gordon suggests that their relationship was not fully established until later in 1959.[29] The anti-nuclear cause was certainly central to the Carters' concerns by the time they married in 1960. Gordon records that Angela even considered writing a 'CND novel' called *And Tomorrow's Doomsday*.[30] The Carters' direct participation with CND continued when they moved to Bristol in 1961. New neighbours who quickly became close friends, Nick and Corinna Gray (née Sargood), were also involved. Nick recalls that he was a 'militant ban-the-bomber' at the time, once sitting down on the steps of the War Office with his mother and Bertrand Russell, while Corinna had been on the Aldermaston marches.[31] Such activism would have helped to establish a bond between the two couples. As we shall see, however, Angela Carter's ongoing attitudes to nuclear disarmament became more complex during her decade in the city.

27 John Minnion and Philip Bolsover, 'Introduction', 9-41 in John Minnion and Philip Bolsover (eds.), *The CND Story: The First 25 Years of CND in the Words of the People Involved* (London: Allison and Busby, 1983), 27.
28 Angela Carter, 'Sugar Daddy' [1983], 19-29 in *Shaking a Leg: Journalism and Writings*, ed. by Jenny Uglow (London: Vintage, 1998), 22.
29 Gordon, *Invention of Angela Carter*, 45-47.
30 Gordon, *Invention of Angela Carter*, 45.
31 Nick Gray, e-mails to the author (4 and 5 June 2018).

Front and back covers from *Songs from Aldermaston* **(co-produced by Paul Carter, 1960).**

The Carters would have known that Bristol was a CND stronghold when they moved to Clifton and would almost certainly have been aware that the Direct Action Committee against Nuclear War had launched a major campaign in the city the previous summer. This was a progressive and ambitious endeavour to appeal directly to industrial workers in the arms industry, attempting to find common cause with local trade unionists at the Bristol Engine Company during a summer-long campaign to promote the peace movement's cause.[32] Bristol-born activist Peter M. Le Mare shared his memories of the anti-war campaigns of this time. The son of a conscientious objector, he became involved in CND as a teenager in the late 1950s, eager to support the opposition to nuclear weapons. He recalled one occasion when he returned from a postering expedition to see a cadets' military vessel moored on the docks at Hotwells. He soon decided to decorate the boat with surplus anti-nuclear posters. A policeman caught him in the act as he was completing his work and he narrowly escaped arrest, partly because he was a youthful eighteen years of age, and partly because the officer was already taking an arrestee back to the station for an unrelated offence. Also, during the late 1950s, Le Mare and his accomplice Douglas Brewood scaled the Avon Gorge

32 Meredith Veldman, *Fantasy, the Bomb, and the Greening of Britain: Romantic Protest 1945-1980* (Cambridge: Cambridge University Press, 1994), 129 (footnote).

to clean up some of the old graffiti and paint a gigantic CND symbol which was visible for many years. Pat Arrowsmith, a key figure in the Direct Action Committee boosted his confidence by inspiring him to stand on a soapbox on Clifton Downs and speak out against nuclear weapons. He was later arrested on a Committee of 100 action during the early 1960s, which resulted in detention in Winchester Prison in Hampshire. Le Mare provides a rare continuity between CND activism in the West Country during the 1950s and the present day.[33]

The Carters, and their contemporaries in the peace movement, both in the 1960s and the 1980s, provide insight into developing cultural responses to nuclear arms. Historian of the peace movement, Richard Taylor, considered the creation of 'a mass extra-parliamentary movement' to have been one of CND's major, and most enduring, achievements.[34] From the outset, music and literature were at the heart of the peace movement, with the relationship between CND and the folk revival being mutually inspirational. Both Pete Townshend and Rod Stewart, singer-songwriters who were to become celebrities from the 1960s onwards, participated in the early Aldermaston marches.[35] Folk musician Ian Campbell recalled that jazz musicians and choirs added a cultural dimension to CND in the late 1950s.[36] Paul Carter had helped to produce the London Youth Choir's record *Songs from Aldermaston*, released in 1960.[37] Campbell also suggested that 'the folk clubs became the places where duffle-coat lapels flaunted CND badges and anti-war songs were assured a

33 Peter M. Le Mare, personal conversation with the author (Bristol, 21 October 2018).

34 Richard Taylor, *Against the Bomb: The British Peace Movement 1958-1965* (Oxford: Clarendon Press, 1988), 340.

35 Pete Townshend as a young banjo playing jazz musician—see Mark Wilkerson, *Who are You: The Life of Pete Townshend* (London: Omnibus, 2009), [Chapter One,, unpaginated]; Nick Groom, 'Union Jacks and Union Jills', 68-87 in *Flag, Nation and Symbolism in Europe and America* by Thomas Hylland Eriksen and Richard Jenkins (Abingdon: Routledge, 2007), 73. Rod Stewart was inspired by Bob Dylan's eponymous debut album, recorded during the period of Dylan's involvement with the civil rights movement: 'I played that first album day and night. When I went on the CND marches at Aldermaston I really thought I was Bob Dylan', Rod Stewart interview with Michael Bonner, 'Never a Dull Moment', *Uncut* (September 2018), 62.

36 Minnion and Bolsover (eds.), *CND Story*, 115-117. George McKay cites The Great Western Marching Band and the Pioneer Jazzmen as two Bristol-based left-wing jazz bands who regularly performed as supporters of CND, anti-Apartheid and other political causes in the late 1950s, early 1960s. George McKay, 'Just a Closer Walk with Thee: New Orleans-Style Jazz and the Campaign for Nuclear Disarmament in 1950s Britain', *Popular Music* 23, no. 2 (2003): 274. There is a photograph of the Pioneer Jazzmen in full swing on an anti-Apartheid march in Park Street, Bristol in the early 1960s in *Recollections of Jazz in Bristol: My Kind of Town*, compiled by Dave Hibberd ([Bristol]: Fiducia Press, 2000), 29.

37 Gordon, *Invention of Angela Carter*, 45.

Campaign for Nuclear Disarmament march, Broadmead, taken by local constabulary in the early 1960s.

sympathetic reception'.[38] As the 1960s began, Angela and Paul Carter devoted much of their energy to both folk music and CND, a combination which would have made Bristol an attractive choice when they moved to the city.

The Carters arrival in Bristol was close in time to the launch of the Centre 42 travelling culture festival. Centre 42 helped the Carters to develop a working relationship and establish a friendship with A. L. Lloyd ('Bert Lloyd') who organised the folk side of the tours. The initiative was the brainchild of playwright Arnold Wesker and a bold attempt to forge a bond between trade unions and left-wing political groups and community performing arts. Centre 42 represented a political dimension to the folk revival, and a cultural dimension to the socialist and peace movement, particularly during the early 1960s. Artist and anarcha-feminist Monica Sjöö (1938-2005) contributed to a Centre 42 exhibition at Bristol's recently opened Arnolfini Gallery in 1962.[39] Christine Molan, folk musician and friend of the Carters, participated in the Aldermaston marches and was on several CND and anti-apartheid demonstrations in Bristol during the 1960s. Molan noted the importance of Centre 42 at this time, commenting:

38 Minnion and Bolsover (eds.), *CND Story*, 116.
39 Rupert White, *Monica Sjöö: Life and Letters 1958-2005* ([s.l.]: Antenna Publications, 2018), 23.

Top: Members of the Bristol and South Western region of the Campaign for Nuclear Disarmament, pictured at Old Market before they left in coaches for Aldermaston.

Left: Two art students, Anna Shepley and Roger Godfrey shelter from the rain during a nuclear disarmament rally organised near Clifton Downs by Bristol Peace Council in 1960.

C42 was deemed an idealistic failure by snooty critics but it brilliantly forged links between folk clubs across the nation, so it got the early '60s folk club guest circuit growing.[40]

While Carter's preoccupations shifted from CND during the 1960s, her interest in nuclear disarmament and the peace movement endured and, as we shall see, came to the fore again during the organisation's 'second wave' from the late 1970s onwards. In 1983 she reminisced fondly about what she considered to have been 'exhibitions of mass sanity', reflecting that: 'Truly, those long gone days of marches from Aldermaston were some of the most moving and beautiful memories of my girlhood'.[41] (This corroborates, incidentally, that she did not attend the first demonstration, since the direction of travel in 1958 was *from* London *to* Aldermaston[42]). She acknowledges, however, that she 'drifted away from CND' after the Cuban Missile Crisis. 1962 was pivotal in thinking about the nuclear threat, being the year when the Cold War realpolitik of the protagonists in NATO and the Soviet bloc notoriously came close to bringing the world to the brink of catastrophe. The armed forces of both superpowers, the Soviets, then the Americans, resumed nuclear testing in 1961.[43] The United States Air Force's provocative siting of medium-range Jupiter nuclear weapons in Turkey, in April 1962, then brought about a further deterioration in international relations when Nikita Khrushchev's Soviet Union countered with a bid to install nuclear surface-to-air missiles in Cuba. When verified, the latter move culminated in the infamously tense diplomatic stand-off, and eventual stand-down, by Khrushchev and J. F. Kennedy in October 1962.

Bob Baker recounted the experience of living through the tensions of the era:

> During the Cuban crisis I remember being on the Downs when things were getting really close and the US Navy went to blockade the Russians. I was with my children on the Downs, my wife and I, and I was wondering which cave I could find to hide in, because of the nuclear attack that was certainly coming[44]

40 Christine Molan, e-mail to the author (25 October 2018).
41 Angela Carter,' Anger in a Black Landscape', 146-158 in *Over Our Dead Bodies: Women Against the Bomb*, ed. by Dorothy Thompson (London: Virago, 1983), 151.
42 Richard Taylor, *Against the Bomb: The British Peace Movement 1958-1965* (Oxford: Clarendon Press, 1988, 29.
43 Taylor, *Against the Bomb*, 77-78.
44 Bob Baker, Skype interview with the author (24 January 2019).

Peter Le Mare also spoke of the febrile atmosphere on the streets in the city centre as international relations deteriorated. At the time of the Cuban Missile Crisis there was a rally down near St Augustine's Parade near Colston Hall. This was addressed by Ronald Sampson, a charismatic speaker from Bristol University. Word got out that the Mayor was having a lavish banquet at the same time. Peter, then just 22, had the loud hailer and somehow calmed people down. The police were intimidating the crowd with dogs which tore his sister's jacket. He recalled that he 'couldn't sing for toffee' but somehow got some singing going and believes that he prevented a near riot.[45] A rare photograph (see above) of an anti-war demonstration passing through Broadmead is likely to have been taken in 1962, in the throes of the Cuban Missile Crisis. Pat Thorne commented: 'We were on that March; I think it was the one where we sat down in the road in Old Market and where Dr Ronald Sampson from Bristol University politics department got arrested'.[46] For many Bristolians, therefore, as for citizens worldwide, the events of 1962 were to be a lasting reminder of the precarious nature of superpower relations in an age of weapons of mass destruction.

It would be a mistake to dismiss Angela Carter's involvement with the peace movement as an ephemeral instance of youthful idealism. Events at the time of the 1962 Missile Crisis caused Carter to rethink her attitudes to the threat of nuclear conflict, but not, she was keen to stress, to adopt the belief in the failsafe deterrent effect of mutually assured destruction, 'the comforting idea that, since the things hadn't been used, they'd *never* be used'.[47] As an internationalist and socialist, she remained unequivocal in her opposition to nuclear weapons. It would be contradictory to be a socialist and to contemplate the strategic massacre of millions of civilian workers using weapons of mass destruction. Gordon, Carter's biographer, asserts that she 'drifted away' (her words), 'disillusioned' (his words) from the movement, following the Cuban Missile Crisis and that by the later 1960s she 'was outgrowing the '"innocent liberal" world of singarounds and CND marches'.[48] Yet the reference to 'innocent liberals' is seemingly from Carter's review of Bob Dylan's recently electrified performances,[49] which makes no mention of CND, beyond allusion to the protest milieu from which Dylan had first sprung. In common with many, the issue of nuclear disarmament was to return to the forefront of Carter's concerns during the second wave of anti-nuclear activism, in the

45 Peter M. Le Mare, personal conversation with the author (Bristol, 21 October 2018).
46 e-mail to the author (10 February 2019).
47 Carter,' Anger in a Black Landscape', 151.
48 Gordon, *Invention of Angela Carter*, 46 and 94.
49 Angela Carter, 'Bob Dylan on Tour', [1966], 323-325 in Uglow (ed.), *Shaking a Leg*, 323.

Vietnam marchers in Bristol city centre, *Evening Post* (31 May 1968).

Advertisement for the Vietnam Folk Concert in Bristol (*Evening Post*, 30 May 1968).

1980s. The cover of Gordon's biography, *The Invention of Angela Carter*, shows the novelist wearing a t-shirt featuring Picasso's stylised dove of peace, a design popularised by the peace movement during the 1980s and possibly even a CND fund-raiser. Carter therefore continued to support the anti-war movement, focusing her attention on the shifting issues that were currently central to public discussion within the wider debate.

From the mid-1960s the escalating war in Vietnam emerged as a more immediate focus of attention for the politically engaged. Astutely, Carter later observed that the human catastrophe in Vietnam came to represent an ideological frontline for sharply conflicting worldviews, not only regarding US foreign policy but for social differences that were even more fundamental. Writing in 1988, she reflected that 'the more I think of it, the odder it seems … that so much seemed at stake in Vietnam, the very nature of our futures, perhaps.[50] While Britain's armed forces did not become directly embroiled in the conflict, despite Harold Wilson's deference to US policy, it became a dominant and divisive social issue. There were local rallies against the war in Bristol as well as the more famous demonstrations in London's Grosvenor Square. Carter may have met some of the young Americans on extended stays in Europe to avoid the draft, who are reported to have frequented the Berkeley Café, one of her favourite haunts, and other cafés in Bristol.[51] In May 1968, a major folk concert against the war sparked significant local controversy

50 Carter, 'Truly, It Felt Like Year One', 212.
51 Dave Lawton, telephone interview with the author (18 January 2018).

as initial sponsors withdrew their support when it became apparent that the event was a fund-raiser to support the National Liberation Front (Viet Cong).[52] Bristolian script-writers, Bob Baker and Dave Martin, whose collaborative work includes contributions to early episodes of *Dr Who* (with the introduction of robotic dog, K9), *Arthur of the Britons*, *Shoestring* and *Wallace and Gromit*, shared the 'outrage'[53] about the ongoing war in Vietnam in the late 1960s. They filmed *Search and Destroy* near Bristol (featuring Keith Floyd, the chef and restauranteur, who was their close friend in Clifton) about the Vietnam conflict. Baker reported that they 'got used to protesting', memorably contributing the script for an anti-Vietnam War production in a London theatre which starred Jane Fonda and the celebrity paediatrician and activist Benjamin Spock.[54] Such interventions underscore the local concern with this issue, in line with the global priority given to the Vietnam War as the leading issue in international relations during the late 1960s and early 1970s.

Opposition to nuclear weapons, the nuclear industry and the war machine continued in the heavily militarised south of England during the 1970s and 1980s. In 1980 the Bristol Anti-Nuclear Group (BANG) staged an audacious action in which activists from Bristol, Bath and Stroud successfully blockaded a train carrying nuclear waste at Sharpness.[55] In 1981, the controversial siting of cruise missiles at Greenham Common and Molesworth exacerbated tensions between the superpowers, instigating another precarious phase of the Cold War. Once more the Wessex region, together with the adjacent county of Berkshire, was in the frontline in the struggle against militarism and the nuclear industry, with targets including the chemical and biological defence establishment at Porton Down, Aldermaston, Burghfield, Hinkley Point and Berkeley power stations, Fairford military air show and the emergency central government headquarters at Corsham. Cruisewatch activists made life difficult for nuclear convoys which attempted to 'melt into the countryside'. During this second wave of mass popular support for CND in the 1980s, the Women's Peace Camp at Greenham Common particularly attracted headlines and considerable international solidarity. In this context, Carter contributed an essay entitled 'Anger in a Black Landscape' to Dorothy Thompson's edited collection, *Over Our Dead Bodies: Women Against the Bomb* (1983). Here she revisited and updated her position on nuclear weaponry, but remained

52 '"Aid for Vietnam" Concert Organiser Hits Back', *Evening Post* (20 May 1968), 2.
53 Bob Baker, *K9 Stole My Trousers: An Autobiography* ([s.l.] Fantom Publishing, 2013), 9. Unfortunately, the film was never completed due to a technical blunder by the team's second cameraman.
54 Bob Baker, Skype interview with the author (24 January 2019).
55 Trevor Houghton, e-mail to the author (28 December 2010).

unequivocal in her opposition to the militarist mind-set, calling upon women to 'rage as if against the dying of the light':

> If the peace movement in Britain *cannot* persuade our (democratically elected) government, this one and the next, to review our position *vis-à-vis* NATO, the establishment of Cruise missiles in this country and our whole relationship with the obscene farce of modern warfare, then perhaps, morally, we do not deserve to survive, and almost assuredly, we will not.[56]

A shift in Carter's thinking is evident by the 1980s, reflecting a development on the part of other anti-nuclear campaigners with internationalist leanings. The emphasis was no longer upon lobbying politicians to appeal to the moral fibre of the British establishment. Now the imperative was to outflank the expansionist ambitions of warring states permanently through the creation of an internationalist federation. New Left socialist David Widgery put it succinctly when reflecting on CND's fortunes in 1976, declaring that 'the only real alternative to mass murder under class rule was workers' control and popular self-government'.[57] Carter acknowledged in 1983 that, after the Cuban Missile Crisis, she had reframed her position, later proposing that:

> [...] The only way to stop nations periodically going to war with one another in this new and morally indefensible way was a concerted impulse towards a federation constructed along humanitarian and egalitarian lines. Given my particular background and bias, this could only mean one thing—international socialism.[58]

Unfortunately, despite honourable but small-scale exceptions, such as the Kurdish freedom movement's ongoing attempts to implement democratic confederalism, efforts to achieve such a federation internationally have not progressed. Carter's point of view, however, has been understood and embraced by sections of the anti-war movement in the 1980s and since. Such

---

56 Carter,' Anger in a Black Landscape',156. The British Library's holdings include a wire from anti-nuclear protests at Greenham Common Airbase, sent to Angela Carter in recognition of her support. British Library Add MS 88899/6/13: [online]: https://www.bl.uk/collection-items/wire-from-anti-nuclear-protests-at-greenham-common-airbase-sent-to-angela-carter [accessed 2 June 2018].
57 David Widgery, *The Left in Britain 1956-1968* (Harmondsworth: Penguin, 1976), 107.
58 Carter,' Anger in a Black Landscape',152-53. Carter adds a parenthetic note that 'international socialism' is not capitalised, thus distancing herself from International Socialism, the Trotskyite forerunner of the Socialist Workers' Party.

thinking was more widely apparent in sections of CND, during the second wave of the nuclear disarmament movement. Reflecting on the 1962 Missile Crisis, Nigel Young commented:

> What we can learn from it in the 1980s is the necessity for a globalist vision of change, a strategy for the longer term, in which the peace movement moves from a negative reactive motivation, towards the empowerment of constituencies which can pre-empt such crises, and re-possess power over political conditions which make such events possible.[59]

This was an important reframing of the existential threat that nuclear weapons represented, embedding an understanding of militarism as a symptomatic expression of the power dynamics of state and capital, to be contextualised within a wider critique of both. Popular nuclear disarmament movements are again at a low ebb, while nuclear, conventional, chemical and biological weaponry has been retained, and in some instances has proliferated, during the ensuing period. The myth of the peace-keeping function of nuclear arsenals is less often challenged in mainstream discourse. Nuclear weapons underpin an inherently destabilising scenario, in which antagonists with the means for mass destruction continue to struggle for power in proxy wars in a context of increasing populations, experiencing exploitation and often displacement, and diminishing resources. Carter was aware of her position as a citizen of the first generation to live with the knowledge of the potential for nuclear obliteration across vast swathes of the planet and realised that, at least in the short-term, humanity would have to come to terms with this predicament. Involvement with the peace movement added breadth to the depth of Carter's

Newsletter from Greenham Common produced in Bristol, with contributions from Pat VT West and Monica Sjöö

59 Frank Allaun *et al.*, 'Problems of the 1960s', 56-67 in *CND Story*, ed. by Minnion and Bolsover, 63.

thought, expanding her planetary vision and providing a context for personal relations. This enabled her to reflect with existential irony upon the human situation and to bring to bear dark humour, a pulse of utopianism, and a practical sense that it was necessary to demythologise the transcendent evil of nuclear weapons if humanity were to avoid being overwhelmed by their presence.

'A Communal Thing': The Folk Revival in Clifton Village

Folk songs are tough, and show an obstinate will to survive. […] It is a curious phenomenon, this revival of folk music as a city music.[60]

I have argued that CND contributed to the latitude of planetary awareness in Angela Carter's ideas. This was complemented by the longitude that folk music supplied, with its historical themes and deep roots, adding richness and dimensionality to her perspective as a writer. As we have seen, Bristol was a significant hub for both the peace movement and the folk scene during the 1960s. Angela Carter, and her then husband Paul Carter, were already active participants in folk music in London in the late 1950s and expanded their involvement in the burgeoning Bristol folk scene[61] when they arrived in the city in 1961. Christine Molan, a key friend and ally in the folk scene at that time, said that Paul, described as a 'folk-loving beatnik' in the *Of Wolves and Women* documentary, 'taught [Angela] (as she said) everything about folk music'.[62] They found their place in their new home, not only as performers but as drivers and developers of the folk revival. Several commentators have recalled that their contributions were considerable. They ran the leading folk label Topic Records, for which they produced and collected songs, started two folk clubs and performed regularly in Bristol and beyond. Most significantly for posterity, Angela's self-development as a professional author unfolded during her quest to understand folk traditions in song, story and dance, and was fuelled by her passion for the folk circles in which she was immersed in these years.

Alongside the works of fantastical art at the 'Strange Worlds' exhibition in Bristol in 2016, there was a small display featuring items linking Angela Carter to the early 1960s folk revival. While much attention has rightly been paid to the lavishly visual qualities of Carter's writing, there is also a significant

---

60 Ralph Vaughan Williams and A. L. Lloyd, Introduction to *The Penguin Book of English Folk Songs* (Harmondsworth, Middlesex: Penguin, 1959), 7.

61 A detailed source is Mark Jones, *Bristol Folk: A Discographical History of Bristol Folk Music in the 1960s and 1970s* (Bristol: Bristol Folk Publications, 2009).

62 Christine Molan, e-mail to the author (26 November 2018).

auditory dimension. As well as the rhythm and cadences sounding out from the prose, there is a soundtrack embedded in each of her early Bristol novels. 'Strange Worlds' featured some of Carter's musical transcripts, the only existing recording of her performing ('The Flower of Sweet Strabane') and a CND folksong programme featuring the Carters' folk club and an advertisement for Ian Campbell 'The Sun is Burning'. Campbell was impressed by the wildfire popularity of his newly written work. His sister Lorna sung the protest song for the first time in London on a Saturday in 1961; by the Tuesday he was astonished to hear 'The Sun is Burning' repeated in Birmingham by someone who had picked it up at a Bristol CND event.[63] Such instances indicate the close-knit networks within CND and the folk movement, a dynamic cultural force through which the Carters could connect more widely as they sought to establish themselves outside of London.

Paul Carter became a director of Topic Records, an independent company with its origins in the 1930s Workers' Music Association and one of the most prominent labels for releases representing the 1960s folk revival. In this capacity, the Carters marketed folk music and went out to capture musical history by collecting and recording material in rural areas in England and both sides of the Irish border.[64] Christine Molan believed Paul Carter was ideally suited to this task, since he approached his work with integrity. She commented that 'Paul was trusted, very aware and far more sensitive than most to the risk of damaging what he'd first set out to preserve'.[65] Gordon Strong met Paul and Angela Carter later in the 1960s due to their mutual acquaintance with the painter Peter Swan. Strong remembered Paul Carter was a considerable expert in Irish folk music.[66] At the end of his life, Paul Carter returned to the folk world, participating in live performances at singing weekends, and was instrumental in the production of a definitive recorded collection of the work of Armagh singer Sarah Makem, initiated by a project to collate previously unreleased material he had recorded for Topic during the 1960s.[67]

Angela Carter increasingly made her own contributions to the folk revival. She wrote the sleeve notes for several of Topic's folk revival albums during

63 Minnion and Bolsover (eds.), *CND Story*, 117.
64 Gordon, *Invention of Angela Carter*, 44. Paul Carter supplied more detail about their activities, while modestly deprecating his role, in some 'Jottings' he supplied at the end of this life in 2012. See: https://www.mustrad.org.uk/obits/p_carter.htm [accessed 17 June 2018].
65 Christine Molan, e-mail to the author (25 October 2018).
66 Gordon Strong, interview with the author (La Ruca Café, Gloucester Road, Bristol 28 February 2019). Strong was also struck by the contrast between Paul Carter's 'quiet, rather taciturn' character and Angela Carter's much more outgoing personality, so was unsurprised that their marriage broke down.
67 Rod Stradling, e-mail to the author (2 December 2018).

Angela Carter provided the sleeve notes for several of Topic Records releases.

the early 1960s. These included two of Peggy Seeger's early EPs, 'Troubled Love' and 'Early in the Spring', both released in 1962. On the back cover of 'Early in the Spring', she paid tribute to Seeger's ability to capture the traditional qualities of the songs she revived, keeping them 'direct and alive' so that it was 'an act of creation not resuscitation'. This indicates Angela's own principles regarding the appropriate treatment of folk heritage. Gordon reports that although she penned an excited diary entry exclaiming 'Peggy Seeger sleeping on my floor', unfortunately, the renowned folk singer had no recollection of Angela Carter.[68] Seeger did, however, recall performing at the Colston Hall during the 1960s, memorable for the great atmosphere and the poor acoustics due to technical equipment that was found wanting.[69] Angela Carter also supplied sleeve notes for 'Ballads and Broadsides' by Louis Killen, a folk singer from Gateshead. She crafted detailed sleeve notes, annotating each of the 'Grand and vigorous story songs' that make up the compendium of Killen's album with its tales of murder, piracy, poaching, sexual violence, a woman who cross-dresses to take part in a naval battle (a significant choice of theme for a folk singer who later self-identified as female), press gangs, a saucy 'night visiting song' and a bittersweet love song.

Paul Carter was involved with live performance soon after the couple moved to Bristol, first singing at the Arnolfini when it was based on The Triangle in Clifton.[70] He quickly decided he wanted to start his own club so, consequently, the Carters founded the 'Ballads and Broadsides' folk club in 1961. This was based at The Bear Hotel in Hotwells Road.[71] There is some controversy about the Carters' approach to folk that embroils them in the

68 Gordon, *Invention of Angela Carter*, 66.
69 Peggy Seeger, response to author's question at Bristol Festival of Ideas event, Peggy Seeger in conversation with Sarah LeFanu at Waterstones, Union Galleries, Bristol (30 May 2018).
70 According to Bob Gale, who met Paul and Angela Carter at this time. Telephone interview with the author (26 November 2018).
71 Ian Anderson in Jones, *Bristol Folk*, 10.

internal differences that were hotly debated within the 1960s folk revival. Bristol-based folk music writer and historian Ian A. Anderson commented of the club: 'We were told that you weren't allowed in with guitars and stuff like that, so we never went there',[72] although he was later to regret the decision. John Hudson, biographer of Fred Wedlock, recounts hostility to the Carters' traditionalist approach, alleging a killjoy, purist line:

> Traditionalists—to a fault, in most Bathurst regulars' eyes—they eschewed anything but unaccompanied singing, and even when they took over the booming Bristol University folk club, they ran a tight ship. Fred always reckoned that Angela, the future novelist, booted him out from there, though in alternative versions of the story his sin was either playing a guitar or singing a funny song that made people laugh.[73]

This account is questionable on three counts. First, because it seems to suggest that Paul and Angela also ran the University club, but I have seen no other source that records this. Second, if the 'alternative versions' of the story are that Fred Wedlock was 'booted out' for playing a guitar or performing humorous songs, this begs the question of what the original reason for his exclusion was. Finally, Angela became a concertina player in 1965, opening, she said, 'a whole new realm of pleasure', and also took up the banjo, so it seems unlikely that they would have enforced a strictly unaccompanied policy, although this may reflect a more relaxed approach at the second club that the Carters ran.[74] Hudson particularly cites Gef Lucena who alleged that when he was running the Poetry and Folk Club:

> [The Carters] occasionally came down and sang, and seemed to take delight in alienating the audience. Once they actually performed with their backs to the room, real finger-in-the-ear stuff.[75]

Molan acknowledged that there were rumours about the Carters' exclusive approach although she challenges their accuracy, drawing attention to the 'all welcome' notice on the Ballads and Broadsides advertisements:

72 In J.P. Bean, *Singing from the Floor: A History of British Folk Clubs* (London: Faber & Faber, 2014), 146.
73 John Hudson, *Fred Wedlock: The Funnyman of Folk* (Bristol: Bristol Books, 2013), 66.
74 Journal entries written on 14 July 1965 and 24 November 1965: British Library Archive: Angela Carter Papers: Journal Add MS 88899/1/90:1965-1966.
75 Hudson, *Fred Wedlock*, 66-67.

Oh yes. Singer-songwriters and protest singers were everywhere in Bristol in the early 60s. It only took one singer to visit B&B for the rumour about 'no guitars' to spread like wild-fire.[76]

Molan said that the CND folk concert that took place on 4th November 1963 at Colston Hall was an occasion to address some of the undoubted differences within the folk revival, commenting:

It was definitely a pivotal moment, an attempt to get all folk factions coming together, [with] illustrious names but for us, Joe [Heaney] stole the show! I expressed surprise at the milling crowds outside the hall, but Angela, who was in the know, murmured to me 'There's no bitchery like folk bitchery'.[77]

Corinna Sargood stayed away from the clubs that her friends had started for different reasons, being put off after a single visit, she said, by 'all those middle-class people singing Durham miners' songs'.[78] This is a shame since for Angela Carter authentic folk embodied a down-to-earth counterblast against the middle-class myth of the 'cold, unemotional' Englishman and Englishwoman.[79] Nevertheless, the clubs attracted some important figures from the folk world, including Bert Lloyd, one of the great pioneers of the folk revival, described by Christine Molan as a 'mentor' to Paul.[80] Susannah Clapp recounted Angela's claim that Ewan MacColl even recorded an interview for one of his celebrated Radio Ballads in their front room.[81] In 1964 the Carters' shifted their location, starting a new venture called the 'Folksong and Ballad' Club at the Lansdown in Clifton.[82] Molan suggests this shift to a new venue was motivated by Paul's desire to establish a club that had a smaller sing-around format which 'was about community, an intimate space to evolve something more creative, which it did'.[83]

76 Christine Molan, e-mail to the author (25 October 2018).
77 Christine Molan, e-mail to the author (25 October 2018).
78 Gordon, *Invention of Angela Carter*, 66.
79 Angela Carter, 'Now is the Time for Singing', [1964], 314-23 in Uglow (ed.), *Shaking a Leg*, 315.
80 Molan, 'Authentic Magic', 30-31. A. L. Lloyd ran 'An Introduction to Folk Song', a series of adult learning classes at the Folk House in autumn 1964, listed in *The English Folk Dance and Song Society: Bristol District* (Autumn 1964), 5.
81 Susannah Clapp, *A Card from Angela Carter* (London: Bloomsbury, 2012), 51.
82 Listings in *The English Folk Dance and Song Society: Bristol District* (Autumn 1964), 5. Also mentioned in Christine Molan, 'Authentic Magic: Angela, Folk Song and Bristol', 29-32 in Mulvey-Roberts and Robinson (eds.), *Strange Worlds*, 29 and 31.
83 Christine Molan, e-mail to the author (25 October 2018).

FOLKSONG AND BALLAD
BRISTOL

This new club, Folk Song and Ballad, Bristol,
meets on alternate Fridays at the Lansdowne,
Clifton Rd., Clifton (buses 17,18,73,83) at
8 p.m.
Membership 1/- Admission 2/- (Guests 2/6)
October 2nd and 16th and subsequent meetings
arranged to avoid clashing with the A.L.Loyd
lectures above. Queries and comments to
N.Curry, 38 Royal York Cresc., Bristol.8.

Listing for the Folksong and Ballad club (published in 1964).

Other reminiscences present warm impressions of the Carters' folk clubs. Anderson spoke of the glowing invitation he received from Paul and Angela to play at the Folksong and Ballad club:

> By this time I was heavily into being heads-down authentic blues. Somewhere around then, trying to prove some long-forgotten point, we'd hauled little amplifiers, a borrowed electric guitar and a bass player down to the Ballads & Blues [Bathurst Hotel] to do a spot, pretending to be Muddy Waters. The Ballads crowd were usually pretty broad minded, but this was too much for them and they hated it and showed it. As we snuck to the back of the room, we spotted Paul Carter (an early director of Topic Records) and his wife Angela (who had not yet become the famous novelist she would later) at the bar. They ran the (reputedly) hardline traditionalist "Folksong & Ballad" club at the Lansdowne [*sic*] in Clifton and if anybody was guaranteed to hate what we'd just done, it would be them. So imagine our surprise when they greeted us warmly, said how much they'd admired the integrity of what we'd just done, and invited us to do a spot at their club. To my regret now, I never dared.[84]

The Carters' friend, the poet Neil Curry was the Secretary for the Club and took the money on the door. He spoke warmly of Paul's 'very likeable' presence in running the club. While paying tribute that 'Angela had a good voice and a wide repertoire', he conceded 'They never let me sing!'[85]

Bob Gale, a Bristol-based artist who moved to Clifton in 1962, was another friend of the Carters at the time, and so also able to give a first-hand

---

84 Jones, *Bristol Folk*, 142. Ian A. Anderson dated this to 1967, e-mail to the author (2 July 2018).
85 Neil Curry, e-mails to the author (3 and 5 October 2018).

account of the Ballads and Broadsides Club and the Folksong and Ballad Club. Gale was a regular at both clubs and was also involved with the Centre 42 project. He would participate on alternate Friday evenings, often continuing at the Royal York Crescent flat afterwards, recalling:

Angela Carter became interested in singing and eventually plucked up enough courage to sing. She had a thin, wiry voice. Bizarrely, they were real purists.[86]

They would make occasional expeditions to other folk clubs in the area. A trip to a pub in the Blagdon area became memorable to Gale due to one of Angela Carter's barbed asides:

A couple with guitars performed. Angela named them 'Piss and Quick'. She could be vituperative. She had her wit, but it was with a rapier tongue. I was naïve at the time and I think this amused them. I'm sure I made gauche comments. I loved wildlife, especially birds, which I think they found bizarre, that I'd go to Brandon Hill to look at birds.[87]

The programme for the major CND folksong concert, held in Bristol's Colston Hall, 4 November 1963, strongly emphasised the intimate crossover between folk music and CND at this time and concluded, 'Folksong is deeply associated with the Aldermaston Marchers, in their mingled cry of protest and hope. In presenting these concerts we hope that more people will come to appreciate, in folksong, one of the good things of living'. The concert was opened by the Ian Campbell Folk Group and included performances from both traditional and protest musicians within the folk scene—the billing listed Bob Davenport, Sandra Kerr, The Haverim, Joe Heaney and Peggy Seeger and Ewan MacColl. This was a notable development. As we have seen, while the Carters' folk clubs were open to all, they had a reputation for being on the traditional wing of the revival. Christine Molan confirmed that 'Paul and Angela were very much in the trad camp as far as folksong goes—neither of them considered the current wave of protest songs as folksongs'. Looking back, she noted the significance of the occasion:

86 Bob Gale, telephone interview with the author (26 November 2018).
87 Bob Gale, telephone interview with the author (26 November 2018). Gale recalled that Paul Carter later became an accomplished ornithologist.

I vividly recall Angela, Paul and several others of us singers all went to the big CND folk concert at the Colston Hall in Remembrance week 1963. An interesting pivotal event—protest singers and trad singers all coming together—for once.[88]

Several commentators have suggested that there are direct and intimate links between the significant place Angela Carter accorded the folk scene in her life during the 1960s, and its contribution to her writing and politics.[89] Folk music was a central preoccupation as she honed her craft through journalism, music reviews, short-story writing and poetry and academic writing before she became a published novelist in 1966. Her master's thesis from the University of Bristol dealt with English ballads and folklore. Molan also paid tribute to Paul Carter's role as 'a quietly pivotal figure in Angela's understanding of oral traditions'.[90] Carter's first published short story, 'The Man who Loved a Double Bass' (1962), is clearly influenced by her early encounters with the London jazz scene before she moved to Bristol. It came first in a short story competition run by *Storyteller* magazine.[91] Music and literary creativity were intimately intertwined in Angela Carter's work. Her passion for music helped her to orchestrate the increasingly melodic style that characterised her prose, her abilities as a writer developed as she explored folk, jazz, rock and other musical genres, and brought alive the sub-cultures from which they sprang.

Carter was well placed to evoke local music scenes in both her fiction and non-fiction because they were part of a world she knew first-hand and valued. In her 1964 essay 'Now is the Time for Singing', she rejected the patronising representation of working-class performers as naïve, charmingly unlettered and spontaneous. To borrow a phrase from E. P. Thompson (whom Carter later knew), she attempted to rescue folk music from the condescension of posterity by drawing attention to its highly stylised and structured qualities. She admired authenticity in performance, and the impressively wide repertoire of some traditional singers. The most outstanding were able to develop their material through an astute synthesis of tradition and creative renewal, recrafting their inheritance so that it retained its emotional charge (a trait she had admired in Peggy Seeger's work). The folk revival was an inherently democratic project discovering and revaluing rank-and-file working-class voices in a way that brought about a reaffirmation of Carter's

88 Christine Molan, e-mails to the author (25 October 2018).
89 Molan, 'Authentic Magic', 30. Edmund Gordon, *The Invention of Angela Carter: A Biography* (London: Vintage, 2017), 44-45.
90 Christine Molan, e-mail to the author (25 October 2018).
91 Gordon, *Invention of Angela Carter*, 64.

socialist principles. With these voices came a strong sense of narrative too, an augmented story-telling tradition that complemented the folk tales and fairy stories that Carter collected and, in some cases brilliantly reworked. Carter's dedication of her second Virago collection of fairy tales to Bert Lloyd is an acknowledgement of the powerful influence of the folk revival on her love of story-telling.[92]

Musical sources and settings inspired much of the content of Carter's work. She drew imaginatively upon some of the visual wonders to be found in the rural, industrial and nautical heritage of folk ballads that are at turns heroic, farcical, tragic, outlandish and bawdy. Gale recalled that 'Angela was always interested in the ballad form with its high-flown, romantic, magical aspects'.[93] The characterisation and milieu of folk and other musical traditions helped to populate Carter's work. Jotted observations on fiddle-players in her personal journal for 1966, for example, which captured encounters on the streets of Bristol, came back in adapted form in her 1967 essay 'A Busker (Retired)', published in *New Society*, reappeared as 'On the Down' in the poetry collection *Unicorn*, and then resurfaced in the character of 'Old Sunny Bannister', a busker in the 1968 novel *Several Perceptions*.[94] The institution of the English pub too, home to countless sessions and singalongs, was to form the mise-en-scène for much of the action in Carter's 1960s novels. *Shadow Dance* features 'The Gloucester' (based on The Greyhound in Clifton) and the magnificently named 'Cornet of Horse', an unnamed bar is the setting for songs and contretemps in *Several Perceptions*, while in the final chapter of *Love* Lee bleakly finds himself with 'two bored lorry drivers playing a fruit machine' in a bar which:

> [...] was a glum and barren place though an old man played upon an out-of-tune piano and a group of exhausted whores now and then broke into song.[95]

Local pubs occupied a central position in the music and countercultural scene of the day. So, what were some of the options open to us, should we have wished to have gone for a night out in one of the characterful establishments frequented by the drinkers, singers and raconteurs who interested Carter in the 1960s or 1970s? In addition to the pubs that hosted the Carters' folk nights,

92 Christine Molan, e-mail to the author (25 October 2018).
93 Bob Gale, telephone interview with the author (26 November 2018).
94 British Library Archive: Angela Carter Papers: Journal Add MS 88899/1/91:1966-1968; Angela Carter, 'A Busker (Retired)', [1967], 325-328 in Uglow (ed.), *Shaking a Leg*.
95 Angela Carter, *Love: A Novel* [1971] (London: Chatto & Windus, 1988), 106.

Bristol could boast of such legendary locals as The Old Duke in King Street, The Albert in Bedminster, The Bathurst Hotel (now the much-loved indie-spot, The Louisiana), and venues such as The Bamboo Club in St Pauls, The Granary, The Locarno Ballroom and the long-running and ongoing Bristol Folk House on Park Street. Each venue would cater for a distinctive clientele and establish a reputation for particular genres of music, thus developing its own in-house ambience and culture.

As the heart of 'provincial Bohemia' in Bristol at the time, Clifton and Hotwells also boasted several significant countercultural venues. The Bristol Troubadour Club, a cramped but hugely popular and much-missed folk venue opened in 1966 in Waterloo Street. The Lion in Cliftonwood, the Quinton House in Park Place and The Adam and Eve, in Hope Chapel Hill, Hotwells, all still serving, were 'alternative' in earlier decades. The Glen, a major live music venue at the top of Whiteladies Road, has long disappeared. The Dugout Club in Park Row has become legendary since it hosted seminal performances by trip-hop musicians such as The Wild Bunch (forerunners of Massive Attack) and Smith and Mighty who came to define the Bristol sound. Carter's friends Dave Lawton and Bob Gale first met in The Somerset in Clifton, less remembered for its musical acts but nevertheless another local institution. The latter described it as 'a drinking club' with a varied clientele, including students, businessmen and prostitutes: 'a Hogarthian centre for everyone. It was very vibrant'.[96]

The Three Tuns in St Georges Road, Hotwells became particularly associated with the emerging beatnik culture from the late 1950s onwards. Peter Le Mare remembered hanging out at the pub with the beatniks at the time, recalling that, while the beatniks didn't spend much money, people would travel to stare at the unconventional clientele with their outrageous hair (the men's hair really just down to their collars) so business picked up for the landlord, who regarded himself as a socialist.[97] The Three Tuns began to attract police attention and was subject to a raid in September 1964 that resulted in eleven arrests. This intervention generated considerable controversy. Gale had friends caught up in the raid who he believed did not smoke drugs. 'This was a very controversial incident. It became a legendary story. Many people were arrested and taken down to the Bridewell'.[98] The allegations that people had cannabis planted on them, suggested in the aftermath of the raid are mentioned in reports in the *Bristol Evening Post* and *The Times,* although

96 Bob Gale, telephone interview with the author (26 November 2018).
97 Peter M. Le Mare, personal conversation with the author (Bristol, 21 October 2018).
98 Bob Gale, telephone interview with the author (26 November 2018).

Ian Vine and Peter Bild, co-editors of *Sixty-Five* which called for an enquiry into the controversial 1964 police raid on Hotwells Beatnik pub 'The Three Tuns' (15 March 1965, *Evening Post*).

'indignantly and strenuously denied by the police officers concerned'.[99] Three University of Bristol students reported the allegations in an article on 'The Three Tuns Affair' in their paper called *Sixty-Five*.[100] The Three Tuns retained its reputation for drugs and as a music venue for several years. Recalling the local folk scene to John Hudson, A.J. Webber said 'Once somebody took me to the Three Tuns which was seen as a bit druggy. It got some good acts, though: I remember playing there once when Donovan was the guest.'[101]

Much of the sense of place based on local pubs is fascinatingly observed in the unpublished journals that Angela Carter kept during her years in Bristol. She particularly liked to watch the characters she saw and heard, and capturing them simply but evocatively in her notebooks. A Saturday night in the Bathurst Hotel, for example, sometime in 1966, is distilled into a brief sketch, not much longer than a haiku:

<u>Downstairs in the Bathurst</u>
Drums & piano with an organ attachment;
2 young men with '50s hairdos;
Sheet music on the piano: 'Distant Drums';
Long table with family party kind of gathering, all singing[102]

The Plume of Feathers in Hotwells (closed 2008) was another favourite pub for singing around the piano and for people-watching, which Angela

99 See report of raid and calls for an inquiry the following year in 'Pub Swoop Beatniks Accused of Having Hemp', *Bristol Evening Post* (22 September 1964), 1; 'I've no Evidence says Police Chief', *Bristol Evening Post* (15 March 1965), 1; [*Times* correspondent], 'Students Press for Inquiry', *The Times* (16 March 1965), 5 [online] *Times Digital Archive*. The quotation is from the *Times* report.
100 'I've no Evidence says Police Chief', *Bristol Evening Post* (15 March 1965), 1;
101 Quoted in Hudson, *Fred Wedlock*, 64.
102 British Library Archive: Angela Carter Papers: Journal Add MS 88899/1/91:1966-1968.

Carter particularly enjoyed. Pat Thorne remembered that she and her husband Dave used to go to this pub regularly with Angela on a Friday night: 'It was an old-fashioned sing-song. It wasn't folk, it was all the songs from the First World War, anything you felt like singing'.[103] In her journal, Carter chronicles a lively night there in 1966:

A folk group, 2 guitars, drums

A plump woman in a very very tight blue cotton dress & she drank gin & lime (which is art, imitating life again)

Old, old songs, 'Putting on the Style', 'When the Saints'

A girl sang, up from the floor, with the full-throated, old-fashioned music hall voice, op art top, short black skirt, dancing, shaking

An old, old man in a cap, possibly the most toothless man in the world, or who ever lived, got up to the microphone & sang 'Goodnight Irene'.

Everybody [illegible] & sings 'I will if you will, so will I' to the tune of She'll be coming Round the Mountain'. [104]

Such hastily scribbled jottings, like Mass Observation recordings copied with a writer's panache, were to inform published pieces such as Carter's 1968 article for *New Society*, 'The Good Old Songs'. Here she celebrated the power of music to affect cultural levelling as she sketched moments of pub life in the 1960s, when characterful singers and musicians from the pre-war era entertained the drinkers, or the wider clientele chorused favourites. Carter found herself living in a singing city, where 'perhaps two-thirds of pubs of any size that have not gone over to musak' and 'even in pubs without music, singing —usually unison but sometimes solo—will break out spontaneously at the saturnalian season of Christmas through to the New Year'.[105] It was heartening for Carter to discover through these outpourings that the society of the spectacle had not entirely replaced community participation. She cherished that pub singing lived on and thrived in the locals and was for the

103 Pat Thorne and Dave Thorne, Skype interview with the author (28 January 2019).
104 British Library Archive: Angela Carter Papers: Journal Add MS 88899/1/91:1966-1968.
105 Angela Carter, 'The Good Old Songs', [1968], 328-332 in Uglow (ed.), *Shaking a Leg*, 329.

most part 'a communal thing'.[106] The songs were promiscuously taken from the hit parade, films and music hall alike, although many people were not endeared by the countercultural heroes of the day:

The massive sophistication of the lyrics of Donovan, Bob Dylan and Lennon and McCartney pass most people by; the singers around the piano don't dig abstruse imagery and hippie allusion.[107] The singers that enthralled Carter were content to take the folk heritage and popular songs they heard and adapt them for their present purposes, forging their own traditions.[108] Happily, although participatory singing for free is now much rarer, such spontaneous singing is not extinct in the present-day city; I have for instance heard customers break into a rendition of 'The Black Velvet Band' and other standards in the pub yard of my local in east Bristol. More commonly, 'Open mic' nights are regularly held throughout the city and thrive.[109]

Carter's early novels reference an eclectic mix of songs and compositions. Given her role as a folk club host and performer, it is unsurprising that folk ballad titles such as 'The Sailor's Lament' and 'The Queen of Northumberland' feature. The song quotations and musical allusions in the Bristol trilogy novels are far from limited to folk, however, but call up a medley of musical genres sung in pubs or played on jukeboxes, including rock'n'roll, classical music, Americana, pop, musicals, blues, hymns and carols. *Shadow Dance* alone is interspersed with tunes including 'Blue Danube', 'Hear that lonesome whistle blow' by Hank Williams, 'My baby sent a letter, addressed it all in red' and 'Oh, it's a long, long while from May to December', a song that Frank Sinatra made one of his standards. A key character in *Several Perceptions*, the busker Sunny Bannister, is a violinist, while additional ambiance is provided by a local rock band called Electric Opera and background characters such as the beatnik

Folk graphic from *Bristol Voice* (August 1976).

106 Angela Carter, 'The Good Old Songs', [1968], 328-332 in Uglow (ed.), *Shaking a Leg*, 329.
107 Angela Carter, 'The Good Old Songs', [1968], 328-332 in Uglow (ed.), *Shaking a Leg*, 331.
108 Much of the value of the folk tradition lies in this continuity and change; see Steve Roud with Julia Bishop, *Folk Song in England* (London: Faber & Faber, 2017), 13.
109 A present-day open mic webpage lists over thirty regularly scheduled open mic nights in Bristol: https://openmicfinder.com/UK/England/Bristol/.

who 'wailed out some snatches of blues on a harmonica'.[110] The dismal events at the denouement of *Love* fittingly unfold to strains of 'Roses of Picardy', a song of doomed love, 'thumped out' on an out-of-tune piano.[111] Such variety of sources add richness to Carter's journalism and fiction through the breadth of musical allusion.

Carter's role as a performer and facilitator, rather than simply a consumer, of music, accounts for the regular appearance of musicians in her novels and the general musicality of her work. Her years in Bristol developed her passion for all kinds of music, and her highly eclectic tastes. She found in the narrative folk tradition a history of struggle, resistance and elegiac sentiment and an invaluable repository of eldritch imagery and local distinctiveness. The ballads also hung upon sensitivity to timing, rhythm, pitch and meter, all essentials in her musical prose. She rapidly recognised the transformational importance of the emerging rock scene, reporting upon performances by Bob Dylan and The Who, and experiencing memorable nights in Bristol's new Mecca Ballroom, The Locarno, where she saw The Who and the Small Faces first hand. But she embraced the less 'cool' popular renditions that she experienced in Bristol's local pubs too, appreciating the social function of the 'communal thing' that they gave voice to.

Bohemianism in the 'Bristol Trilogy'

'[Shadow Dance] didn't give exactly mimetic copies of the people I knew, but it was absolutely as real as the milieu I was familiar with: it was set in provincial Bohemia'.[112]

Angela Carter wrote her first five published novels during the years that she lived in Bristol. Although Bristol is not named as such, three of these (*Shadow Dance* (1966), *Several Perceptions* (1968) and *Love* (1971)) are set in the city and considered as the 'Bristol Trilogy', following Marc O'Day's designation

110 Carter, *Several Perceptions*, /9. The band was originally to be called 'Dream City', initially conceived as a '"Loving Spoonful"-type group, gay, hip & off-hand', but Carter later considered that the 'Byrds number "8 Miles High" is just the thing "Dream City" would do', reflecting the rapidly developing psychedelic sounds of the times. British Library Archive: Angela Carter Papers: Journal Add MS 88899/1/90:1965-1966.
111 Carter, *Love*, 106-107.
112 Angela Carter quoted in O''Day, '"Mutability is Having a Field Day": The Sixties Aura of Angela Carter's Bristol Trilogy,' in *Flesh and the Mirror*, ed. by Sage, 24. She also acknowledged that 'I was twenty-five when I wrote [*Shadow Dance*] and most of the characters were based on my friends and I myself had genuinely thought of it as a naturalistic novel', Angela Carter, 'Notes on the Gothic Mode', *Iowa Review* 6.3 (Summer-Fall 1975), 132.

The Who at Colston Hall, 24 June 1964. Angela Carter met and interviewed the band when they returned to Bristol to play at the Locarno Ballroom in 1966.

© BRISTOL POST

© BRISTOL POST

'Bowling at the New Bristol Centre', 12 February 1967. This new complex opened in 1966 and included the Locarno Ballroom, where Angela Carter briefly worked, and which features in her novel, *Love*.

as such.[113] In contrast to many of Carter's later novels and short stories, these early works are embedded in a specific time and place, since when she drank in the local alehouses, she imbibed the local culture too. The result is a synthesis of locally distinctive elements, that characterise the neighbourhood of Clifton Village, with the profound changes that were taking place in the global village.

Shadow Dance

In *Shadow Dance*, much of the action takes place in a local pub called 'The Gloucester'. This is based upon The Greyhound, which continues as a bar and music venue, now renamed The Bristol Fringe, at 32 Princess Victoria Street, Clifton. Gordon describes the pub's clientele in the 1960s as 'largely made up of aspiring writers, out-of-work actors, penniless painters and musicians'.[114] The landlord in the 1960s, who was called Peter, was Polish and believed to have been a fighter pilot in the Second World War. For regular Bob Gale 'The Greyhound was a great potpourri of people and a meeting place for everybody. You could always go there, and you would meet people you knew'.[115] Dave Lawton, a member of the University of Bristol Physics Department during the 1960s, also knew Angela and Paul Carter and socialised with them at The Greyhound. *Shadow Dance* has coded references to local characters, Lawton reveals. 'She was a beautiful girl, a white and golden girl, like moonlight on daisies',[116] for example, referred to a local woman:

> …known as the Clifton flasher. All she used to wear was a raincoat. One time she flashed me while I was sitting on a bar stool in the Greyhound pub. She swivelled around on her stool and opened her raincoat flashed and swivelled back again and carried on drinking. That was [X] for you, one of the great characters of Clifton.[117]

Neil Curry also recognised people and places he knew in the novel since he 'detected shades of his first wife in *Shadow Dance*' and identified the original for the waitress that Carter unkindly characterised as the 'Struldbrug' (in allusion to immortal beings that continue to age in Jonathan Swift's *Gulliver's Travels*): 'the Struldbrug often had a ciggie in her mouth while wiping down

113 O'Day, '"Mutability is Having a Field Day": The Sixties Aura of Angela Carter's Bristol Trilogy,' in *Flesh and the Mirror*, ed. by Sage.

114 Gordon, *Invention of Angela Carter*, 61.

115 Bob Gale, telephone interview with the author (26 November 2018).

116 Carter, *Shadow Dance*, 3.

117 Dave Lawton, private Facebook message to the author, 12 October 2017.

our tables with a wet rag as a sign that we'd been there long enough'.[118] This also corroborates that The Berkeley—and Curry recalls that 'The Burk' was 'a bit scruffy'—was the model for the café in *Shadow Dance* which leading character, Morris Gray regularly visits:

> When Morris first came to the town, the back-room self-service cafeteria of this café was panelled in grained wood and the chairs and tables were solid and immovable oak. Everything had been a nutritious brown, then. The slow years passed.
>
> As they passed, the management family decided to drag the place by its ears into contemporaneity. It was forced, against its will, to become a coffee bar.[119]

The human geography that for the most part marks the terrain of *Shadow Dance* is approximately two miles square in the Clifton and Hotwells area. The characters that dwelt within this area in the mid-1960s are defined by their spatial and temporal environment and, in turn, give the neighbourhood its character. The scale of the counterculture was, of course, smaller in Bristol, more concentrated and parochial than strongholds in London such as Notting Hill or Camden and Kentish Town, which for example, had a higher concentration of squatted properties than anywhere in the country.[120] Indeed, Carter suggests the members of the micro-community in Clifton had more than face-to-face familiarity with each other. She is said to have speculated of The Greyhound that 'Everybody in this pub has been to bed with everybody else'.[121] The chief protagonists in *Shadow Dance*, Ghislaine and Honeybuzzard, are both characterised by their promiscuity. When Ghislaine first enters 'The Gloucester' we are told about her sexual history with most of the men who were regulars at the bar. Lawton is confident that she is based on none other than the regular in The Greyhound who had once 'flashed' at him.[122] Ghislaine's experience

118 Neil Curry, e-mails to the author (3 and 5 October 2018).
119 Carter, *Shadow Dance*, 29.
120 By the early 1970s, the alternative society in the latter had developed its own extensive infrastructure. See Stephen E. Hunt, *The Revolutionary Urbanism of Street Farm: Eco-Anarchism, Architecture and Alternative Technology in the 1970s* (Bristol: Tangent, 2014), 72 and Alexander Vasudevan, *The Autonomous City: A History of Urban Squatting* (London: Verso, 2017), Chapter 2.
121 Gordon, *Invention of Angela Carter* (interview with Corinna Sargood, 10 December 2012), 61. Possibly, the fact that the prototypes for the characters are identifiable by those in the know in this sexually close-knit neighbourhood is one reason why Carter never names Bristol in her anonymised fictional city.
122 Dave Lawton, telephone interview with the author (18 January 2018).

makes it apparent that this close-knit neighbourhood not only features convivial elements of cosy familiarity and community solidarity, but also harbours alienation, ostracism and abuse. Carter's account of the provincial bohemia she found in Bristol is refracted through the perspective of the conflicted and complicit figure of Morris and is marked by fascination but not celebration.

Carter was alert to the dysfunctional, contradictory aspects of alternative society. Honeybuzzard, whose personality and activities are the dominant focus of interest, is a protean sociopath.[123] It is he, not the colourless Morris Gray, that is the eponymous shadow dancer. Off his multifaceted character darkness and light glance and flicker like a human glitterball that alternately attracts and repulses all around. Honeybuzzard is a superficially charismatic character with energy and abundant imagination. Honeybuzzard's zest for life, cultural dilettantism and brutality make him a match for the sadistic Alex in Anthony Burgess's 1962 novel, *A Clockwork Orange* (Burgess and Carter became regular correspondents). Having at once a 'water-melon-slice grin'[124] and lethal curare ring, he is assumed to have slashed and violently disfigured Ghislaine's face. He is egocentric to the extent that he regards others as but shadows, which he, as a song and dance man, casts and manipulates at will, yet ultimately Carter's depiction of Honeybuzzard is the study of an existential creature who has no centred being at all. His fantasies of power skip along a thin line between theatrical whimsy and terror:

> I would like to be someone different each morning. Me and not-me. I would like to have a cupboard bulging with all different bodies and faces and choose a fresh one every morning. And spike a rose in the buttonhole, yes. There was a man, last night; we were in a club and there was this man, singing blues, and he had a red rose in his shirt. It was red as a cap of liberty… I would like to wear him, tomorrow morning.[125]

With his imagined cupboard of compliant, disembodied bodies, Honeybuzzard's narrow concept of self-liberation is to be achieved only at the expense of others. He desires another man's red rose, red like the Phrygian cap, but admires it only through the denial of the agency of its wearer and by fantasising that he confiscated the man's presence and somehow engulfed him within his own demeanour. This refusal of others' autonomous expression

123 Gordon notes that he is reputedly loosely based on Carter's acquaintance John Orsborn, *Invention of Angela Carter*, 80.
124 Carter, *Shadow Dance*, 88.
125 Carter, *Shadow Dance*, 78.

results in a lust for control that is fascistic rather than emancipatory:

> I should like,' said Honey dreamily, 'to have a floor set out in chequers and to play chess with men and women. I would stand on a chair and call out my moves from a megaphone and they would click their heels and march forward.[126]

As such Carter was aware of the enduring tension between the necessary, creative impulse for individual expression, and aspirations for collective liberation; potentially divergent energies that the 1960s counterculture struggled to integrate and reconcile. The exhilarating hedonism Carter found, and more importantly experienced, among Clifton bohemia provided opportunities to explore such fault-lines with increasingly powerful dramatic effect.

As decolonisation advanced, the sun literally set for the last time on substantial swathes of the British Empire during the 1960s. The home countries, however, enjoyed prosperity and the welfare state provided a level of security from absolute want. For much of British society, there was a circumscribed, and as it turned out temporary, period of relative economic security and peace. Despite the ongoing Cold War and proxy wars that raged in the developing world, closer to home there was an absence of military conflict, at least until the Irish War broke out at the decade's close. The end of compulsory national service in 1963 was symbolic of better times. Longstanding injustices, derived from the class system, gender and ethnic disparity, were challenged. Corporate power was burgeoning, yet its hold over governance had not yet been consolidated. Surveillance may have been entrenched, but control mechanisms were less than efficient, and the phenomenon of big data was not to fully develop, with its benefits and perils, until the following century. Above all, this was a high point of popular capitalism for many who looked forward to the prospect of abundance and a standard three-day week, assumed to be ahead in the 1970s. While intermittent periods of boom and bust were still expected, what was not anticipated was that the era would be succeeded by an ongoing neo-liberal experiment, that promised wealth creation, but was to fail so bleakly, enduringly, comprehensively and devastatingly due to its endemic contradictions, as it exacerbated social divisions, inequality and environmental destruction.

In the context of the affluent society, there were enough niches within which bohemians could thrive on low incomes, whether in urban areas or by settling on cheap land in rural areas. For the characters in *Shadow Dance*, Bristol's fading grandeur was both a material resource and a kind of playground

126 Carter, *Shadow Dance*, 117.

for the imagination. For the prominent figures such as Gray, Honeybuzzard and Ghislaine, the divide between work and recreation is a narrow one since they are self-employed or get by in the informal economy rather than by earning wages. During the late 1960s and 1970s it was axiomatic that increasing automation would lead inexorably to a shorter working week. If the longer-term prospects were darkening for a nation in decline, but there was more discretionary time available, why not dance in the shadows?

Behind the transparent vitrines of Morris's and Honeybuzzard's antique shop front, most transactions fittingly take place in the shadow economy. Their forays to search for items of bric-à-brac that they can salvage and sell are part business ventures, part playful treasure hunts and part looting expeditions.[127] There was an emerging affection and demand for what had previously been designated as Victorian 'rubbish'. At the risk of overgeneralising, in the 1940s there were more pressing matters to consider, in the later 1950s the prevailing preoccupation is likely to have been with growing prosperity and innovation after the years of rationing and austerity, while the 1960s came to be associated with self-discovery, exploration and experimentation. By the later 1960s, the nineteenth century was far enough back in time to gain an aura of exoticism and otherness and Victoriana began to become desirable.[128] From the early 1970s, Edward Fletcher and others popularised treasure hunting and bottle collecting. This was a pastime that demanded the thrilling combination of exploration, documentary investigation and scrub-bashing with a fresh appraisal of the artistry of rubbish. It led to an interest in social history and joy in material objects that was distinct from consumerist acquisitiveness. In the spirit of this levelling aesthetic, public archaeology became attractive to those with an intuitive alertness to the vulgar topography of derelict buildings and rural rubbish dumps, betrayed by bumps and nettlebeds down rutted greenways.

Positively, the increasing appreciation of Georgian, Regency and Victorian architecture inspired several concerned individuals and societies to contest threats to the built environment. Most notable were attempts to preserve the Kingsdown and Totterdown districts of Bristol from the wrecking ball.[129]

127 O'Day beautifully applies Michael Thompson's theories on the economic value of 'rubbish' to Morris and Honeybuzzard's forays into Victorian dereliction in 'Mutability is Having a Field Day', 33-40.
128 Nevertheless, the Victorian era was not so remote either. Those of us born in the year *Shadow Dance* was published, 1966, were still dandled by grandparents born in the Victorian and Edwardian era. Indeed, the last Victorian born in the British Empire, supercentenarian Violet Brown, died in Jamaica, in September 2017.
129 For an account of the 'act of civic vandalism' in Totterdown and the community opposition it provoked, see Kate Pollard, *Totterdown Rising: A Story of Endurance and Survival* (Bristol: Tangent, 2006).

Possibly the derelict William Square of *Shadow Dance* was based upon Dowry Square, a stone's throw from The Bear in Hotwells. This was the location of the Pneumatic Institute, where Thomas Beddoes and Humphry Davy had formerly enjoyed their celebrated experiments with laughing gas in the parlour of a fine early-Georgian house. By the 1950s, Dowry Square was a site of semi-dereliction until architect Peter Ware (1929-1999) and others began to promote substantial renovation work.

In the absence of surveillance, areas of empty premises and dilapidation also generated opportunities for the likes of Morris and Honeybuzzard to salvage and repurpose loose items, fixtures and fittings that might otherwise have been destroyed. The availability of such items was to support a growing number of reclamation yards, enabling an alternative economy based on recycling. The situation could also be exploited, however, as historical artefacts and street furniture were plundered to meet the demands of wealthier residents, just as gatherers of ferns and seaweed collectors had at one time ransacked the woods and shores of nineteenth-century England and colonial venturers had looted the ancient heritage of subaltern territories to satisfy the desires of Victorian connoisseurs.[130] In the case of William Square, the properties are vacant because the tenants have been recently turned out against their will. This indicates a lack of class solidarity on the part of Honeybuzzard and Morris, who are happy to make money looking for 'American-bait' to sell in their shop at the expense of their evicted neighbours. While profit may have been an initial motive, however, it becomes secondary to pleasures stimulated in yet more sinister reaches inhabited by the human psyche. On Carter's pages, the nocturnal expeditions are brilliantly executed voyages into the abject, marked by filth and savagery. This is Gothicism transposed to the late twentieth century. Horror is enacted not in the vaults of medieval castles, but rendered accessible, affordable and inclusive, made up of elements such as 'predatory' domestic cats, 'night air thick and brown and heavy as cocoa', newspaper clippings of yesteryear's murders, a 'raped doll' that has been stripped and stabbed (surely echoing the violation of the child-like Ghislaine) and 'an excrement choked lavatory' in a 'malignant' house with a 'horrid will'.[131] Throughout, there is an undercurrent of

130 Bristol City Council provoked a mini-scandal in the city in 2008 when Victorian street lamps were removed, without consultation, from St Andrews and re-sited in the wealthy Clifton area. Caught red-handed, the Council unconvincingly defended the lamp-grab on the grounds that it 'offered good value to all tax payers'. See Richard Savill, 'Victorian lamp-posts removed from Bristol suburb and placed in more fashionable areas' *Daily Telegraph* (5 June 2008): https://www.telegraph.co.uk/news/uknews/2080282/Victorian-lamp-posts-removed-from-Bristol-suburb-and-placed-in-more-fashionable-areas.html [accessed 30 June 2018].
131 All references in this paragraph are to Carter, *Shadow Dance*, Chapter 6. The idea of an evil house is perhaps influenced by the theme of the popular horror film *The Haunting*, released in 1963.

voyeurism, given the chances their trespasses give them to glimpse into the intimate lives of others:

> There was the pleasure of creeping through the abandoned dark, of prying and poking. And if that was the real motive for these excursions, then they kept it even from each other and cherished the pleasure separately.[132]

'Pretty Tomorrow' and Several Perceptions

By 1967, hippies were becoming a familiar sight in Clifton: men in kaftans, women with flowers in their hair; Angela called them the papillons dorées—the gilded butterflies. If there was a pinch of irony in her attitude towards them, she also identified with their ostentatious refusal to conform.[133]

In 1966, despite mood swings marked by periodic bouts of depression, there were moments when Carter was buoyed up by the infectious optimism and fluid possibilities all around. She had an impetus to capture the spirit of the times, sketching out plans to write a novel that would paint 'a picture of the popular culture of a provincial city'. This was, of course, Bristol. Considerations for the title of her pop novel included 'Good Times', 'The Joy Kids', 'A Week's Night Out', 'Play-Times', 'Joy Times' and, most promisingly, 'Pretty Tomorrow', all of which speak of the hopeful and upbeat sense of ongoing festivity in the city.[134] Carter intended the novel to be 'Loose, almost plotless in structure', listing the contents as:

Discotheques
Clubs
Wrestling
Pop concerts
Pub music
Etc etc etc
Ice rink
The cats

132 Carter, *Shadow Dance*, 90.
133 Martin Hoyle to Edmund Gordon (7 April 2012), *Invention of Angela Carter*, 106.
134 All references to 'Pretty Tomorrow' are from: British Library Archive: Angela Carter Papers: Journal Add MS 88899/1/90:1965-1966.

She wrote exuberantly: 'Maybe because I'm happy, now and suddenly, I want 'Pretty Tomorrow' to be a really gay kind of book, a book of delights—I can leave the doom until I'm older'. Unfortunately, Carter's euphoria was short-lived, and the fortunes of the novel were subject to her own shifting well-being. She scribbled next to her plans for the novel 'This one died at about the fifth month, it was a total miscarriage', a comment that is highly charged since Carter also expressed a frustrated desire to have a baby at this time. As an author Carter needed more grit and resistance in her narrative than light hedonism could afford to sustain literary tension and interest. Furthermore, the social optimism in Bristol was surely more fragile than the delights of 'Pretty Tomorrow' would suggest.

Written in 1967, *Several Perceptions* (published in 1968), the next novel that was to reach full-term, therefore, included some of the ideas and sketches for 'Pretty Tomorrow' but was more nuanced in its sense of optimism. Gatherings and expeditions in Bristol, and particularly around Clifton, similarly ground the action in this second novel in the trilogy. In *Several Perceptions*, the chief character, Joseph Harker, 'a right little beatnik',[135] drifts outside of the formal economy, much like his counterparts in *Shadow Dance*. Written during the summer of love, *Several Perceptions* is more embedded within the 1960s counterculture and has more elements of local distinctiveness than *Shadow Dance*. Again, neither Clifton or Bristol are explicitly mentioned, yet the view from Joseph's leaky garret, is a neat prospect of the city in vignette:

> At the foot of the hill of crescents and terraces flowed the river with a barge or boat upon it; here the city dock and all the cranes and warehouses reflecting themselves in stretches of dark water; there white lines of the flyover buzzing with traffic; the prim red inexpressive grids of housing estates; and surrounding everything a rim of sweet green hills.[136]

The narrative of *Several Perceptions* tends towards utopianism, in contrast to *Shadow Dance* which starts and ends with dystopian elements. The characters in both novels take part in exploits which are exhilarating acts of trespass, although to different effect. Both novels end in rites of a pagan nature, but the direction of the journey, if there is indeed any trajectory, is divergent. *Shadow Dance* moves towards a human sacrifice as the ill-fated Ghislaine is laid out as a decorative corpse. *Several Perceptions* begins with an alienated and suicidal Joseph Harker, moves through an initially ambivalent act of liberation at the

135 Angela Carter, *Several Perceptions* (London: Virago, 1968), 112.
136 Carter, *Several Perceptions*, 14.

centre of the novel and concludes with an idyllic coming together that glows with reconciliation and hope.

Joseph attempts to raise his own self-worth by making an impact through what would be known later as random acts of kindness. His poverty at the novel's outset is partly due to his generosity in giving money to beggars. Later, Joseph conspires with Kay Kyte, a chance accomplice and fellow beatnik whom he initially dislikes, in the audacious liberation of a badger from the local zoo.[137] Anthropomorphising, Joseph explicitly identifies with the badger in his predicament. From Joseph's perspective, even though the badger is mad with fury and desperation his spirit of resistance against his incarceration is admirable. It is preferable to the quiescence of his co-captives such as the 'smug gorillas' and the black panther who seem to Joseph to have come to terms with their imprisonment, demonstrating a kind of non-human Stockholm syndrome. For Joseph, the direct action involved in breaking into the zoo to take and set the creature loose, is a refusal of his own hopelessness and is an existential exercise in sense-making.[138] In Joseph's mind, there is a link between the escapade with the badger and an earlier suicide attempt, causing him to confide to Kay 'I tried to clip my way out of the cage of flesh but had a spectacular failure'.[139] Whether Joseph's act of kindness will be successful, for the well-being of the badger or for his own self-therapy, remains to be seen. Just as they cannot be certain that the badger will survive and thrive, Joseph's well-being remains fragile and provisional. Nevertheless, the moment of liberation is described as positively intoxicating and euphoric, since Joseph and Kay experience success which leaves them feeling ecstatic. The episode on Clifton Downs illustrates several prevailing aspects of the bohemian mind, namely the reassessment of institutions such as the zoo, the power of redemption through positive action and the imaginative creation of peak experiences in the here and now.

The Vietnam War forms a global backdrop to the parochial incidents in Joseph's life and neighbourhood and is a counterbalancing preoccupation for him. The cataclysm and atrocities of Vietnam even encroach at the subconscious level.

> Every minute of the lonely nights was filled with dreams of fires quenched with blood and bloody beaks of birds of prey and bombs blossoming like roses with bloody petals over the Mekong Delta.[140]

137 Angela Carter took on a temporary catering job at Bristol Zoo, on Clifton Downs, during the 1960s.
138 A similar act of liberation forms the centrepiece of Russell Hoban's wonderful 1975 novel *Turtle Diary*.
139 Carter, *Several Perceptions*, 59.
140 Carter, *Several Perceptions*, 4-5.

Like his relationship with his kindred spirit, the badger, the external reality of the conflict in South-East Asia is conflated with Joseph's interior disturbance, precipitating 'audial hallucination'.[141] His relationship with the war is ambivalent in as much as he is obsessed with the conflict from afar, because it is mediated through snippets of newspaper cuttings and snatches of radio broadcasts. The accusations of Joseph's therapist, Ransome, may be correct:

> I don't think you care at all about the sufferings of the people of Vietnam, Joseph; not in any real sense of involvement with a real situation. You make no move to relieve those sufferings in any real way, through voluntary service, for example. You don't even join in any organized protest. Rather, you've taken this dreadful tragedy of war as a symbolic event and you draw a simple melodramatic conclusion from this complex tragedy—you use it as a symbol for your rejection of a world to which you cannot relate. Perhaps because of your immaturity.[142]

Here, Ransome is likely to be displacing his own ineffectual response to the situation. He may also, however, be reflecting something of the national psyche, as the population of the recently dominant colonial power looked on from the sidelines, at once relieved to be at a distance and appalled. Britain's armed forces did not directly intervene in the savage reality of the faraway theatre of war. Yet, as mentioned earlier, Carter later mused on the immense symbolic weight that the Vietnam War came to carry, representing a colossal rift in a society in which a purported post-war consensus was beginning to fragment. In 1985, ten years after the war's end, Angela Carter considered the decision to call back the military from Vietnam to have been America's 'finest hour', since anti-war opinion had mobilised to such effect, that the continuation of the conflict, with its disastrous impact evident to all, had been rendered politically untenable.[143]

Despite the context of global conflict and characters who are living lives of desperate alienation at the local level, *Several Perceptions* charts the possibility for change and the potential for a transition to a more empathetic future society. Again, this is a departure from the sinister, Machiavellian undertones that pervade much of *Shadow Dance*. Joseph is encountered as psychologically

141 Carter, *Several Perceptions*, 35.
142 Carter, *Several Perceptions*, 63-64.
143 'Angela Carter talks to Lisa Appignanesi' [1985] https://www.youtube.com/watch?v=SrrEdWNP1rk [accessed 23 November 2018].

fragile and as an outsider, who comes to ponder, 'Do you really think I should clamber back into society?'[144] Similarly, Anne Blossom first appears as a tragically isolated character who 'wore a heavy veil over her personality',[145] yet, in keeping with her name, begins to blossom and find resilience, dramatically discovering hope through simple human contact as the novel develops. From Carter's later reflections on the period, it seems that something was going on that created a rare moment of cultural optimism, a provisional and fragile moment that was gestured towards in the pages of this 1967 novel.

The conclusion to *Several Perceptions* best evokes the kind of 'festal' feeling that Carter expressed in her description of late 1960s Bristol. The denouement is structurally reminiscent of Shakespeare's final plays, with their powerful spirit of reconciliation. The leading, and for the most part alienated, characters come together to celebrate the festive season in the decaying mansion where Kay Kyte lived with his mother. Moments of chaos and tenderness ensue. There is a heady ambience made up of sex, incense, fancy dress, church bells, birdsong and sparklers, with a backdrop of a live set by local band Electric Opera succeeded by Sunny the busker's performance, which lulls all with his unexpectedly beautiful violin music. Symbolically the occasion is the Winter Solstice, described as 'one of the numinous hinges of the year',[146] radiant with the purifying forces of icy weather and blazing fires. The night turns into a time of healing and new beginnings as rivalries, psychic burdens and insecurities are eased. The enchanting evening seems to suspend time. With its elements of masquerade, in which characters are bedecked with peacock feathers and daisy chains, the gathering is likely to be a temporary hiatus in human suffering but is no less profound since the powerful moments of secular epiphany will have consequences into the new year and years to follow.

Having kindly blessed her creations with a happy ending, perhaps uncharacteristically, it is necessary to account for this happiness. The answer, it would seem, lies in a subtle fusion of happenstance and the fact that the lead characters, under the intensity and intoxication of the occasion, are willing to step outside of their usual roles, becoming, for example, willing to forgive (Viv tolerates the infidelity of his girlfriend Rosie and best friend Joseph) and to experiment (Anne Blossom leaves her dreary basement and surprises Joseph by staying the course of the party). Kay Kyte and Anne make sacrificial votive deposits, as they respectively consign a picture of Kay's domineering late father and Anne's ring of one-time love, together with a lock of her lost baby's hair into the flames, taking with them life-denying feelings of fear and guilt. Most

---

144 Carter, *Several Perceptions*, 125.
145 Carter, *Several Perceptions*, 46.
146 Carter, *Several Perceptions*, 143.

magically of all, Anne then transcends her disability by walking gracefully, then 'exultantly' without a limp, seemingly by the force of collective good will, until this once taciturn and emotionally absent woman starts, miraculously, to run 'rippling with laughter like a quiet brook'.[147] When Joseph returns to a feline nativity scene, discovering his cat has given birth to 'five kittens all as white as snow and beautiful as stars', the enchantment is likely to be short-lived, since we know that, compelled by circumstances, he is likely to act on his resolution to take the kittens away.[148] Nevertheless, the fragile and temporary nature of the solstice events, described as a voyage on a 'magic ship of light' makes them no less valuable or authentic. Nowhere does Carter evoke more keenly the provisional yet 'festal' behaviour in the Clifton bohemia of the late 1960s.

Carter was an admirer of the brilliant novelist and philosopher John Cowper Powys, a writer who made happiness core to his sense-making in human lives typically marked by challenge and suffering. Powys considered that whenever someone can secure pleasure or happiness by snatching a 'secret joy' in defiance of evil, that moment, however trivial, has cosmic significance. This is based on the premise that there will never be another time when that someone, once he or she has been born, will not have existed. He asserts that 'to enjoy the unfathomable pleasure which your soul half-creates and half-discovers, you have added something to the reality of existence *which will always remain*'.[149] The phenomenon of happiness, therefore, becomes a topic of interest and profound meaning in its own right.

The style and content of *Several Perceptions* perhaps anticipate the kind of writing which was later routinely to cause Carter's work to be labelled magical realism. More significantly for my present argument, it was also deeply rooted in the circumstances of its composition, wrapped around its time and place in 1960s Clifton like ivy, one of Carter's effective metaphors for closeness and intimacy in *Several Perceptions*:

> Orange russet locks of Barbie's hair crept like ivy over Anne's arms and throat for the accident of sleep brought them close as lovers.[150]

---

147 Carter, *Several Perceptions*, 145.
148 A journal entry written in April 1966 shows that Carter intended to include an entire chapter which, intriguingly, would consist of her protagonist just 'looking at the world as a cat, crawling about the floor at cat level': British Library Archive: Angela Carter Papers: Journal Add MS 88899/1/90:1965-1966.
149 John Cowper Powys, *Key to Happiness* [1937], 42.
150 Carter, *Several Perceptions*, 147.

Love

While inhibitions are successfully suspended to usher in connection and trust in *Several Perceptions,* the sense of the 'festal' was not to win out in the final novel in the Bristol trilogy. Written in 1969, *Love* was a return to the darker atmosphere abroad in the 1960s, a critique of the contradictions and the dysfunctional, anti-social aspects of the counterculture, a theme explored by other means in *Shadow Dance*. Although they are living in the late twentieth century, the world-views of the bohemians in *Love* can be radically anachronistic. Annabel Collins is particularly superstitious, interpreting the world according to a 'system of correspondences',[151] reminiscent of a medieval world view and ultimately a part of her self-destructive fatalism. Fantasy and fatalism also pervade the reality of her husband, Lee Collins, a school teacher who is ostensibly more grounded than his emotionally disturbed wife. Yet Lee too divines the cosmos according to paranormal perspectives, at one time experiencing the presence of his brother as 'a giant, hairy toad squatting upon his life and choking him'. His attraction to, and rationale for marrying, his wife was:

> [...] Because he was unsure of his effect upon her and became increasingly attached to her because of her strangeness which seemed to him qualitatively different but quantitatively akin to the strangeness he himself felt, as though he could say of the world: 'We are strangers here.' Fish in the sea are luminous so that they can recognize each other; might not men and women also exude some kind of speechless luminescence to those akin to them?

The claim that Lee 'had never been superstitious in his life before',[152] moreover, is belied by several earlier encounters, which include meeting a boy whose recurring presence imbues his reality with meanings from tarot and 'a feeling of foreboding' when the same boy offers to replace his lost wedding ring with a moonstone ring.[153]

Recalling the sociopathy of Honeybuzzard, the characters in *Love* are alienated and either lack the capacity to imagine the agency and volition of others or positively enjoy exploiting such agency for their own gratification. As an artist, Annabel prepares rather meticulously for her suicide, fittingly a creative endeavour, but 'she did not spare a thought or waste any pity on

151 Carter, *Love*, 1.
152 Carter, *Love*, 97.
153 Carter, *Love*, 68.

the people who loved her for she had never regarded them as anything more than facets of the self she was now about to obliterate'.[154] Lee's brother Buzz, marked by 'merciless self-absorption' also lacks empathy. One of the first things we learn about Buzz is that he 'liked organizing parties for he always hoped something terrible would happen when so many people intersected upon one another'.[155] Again Carter gestures towards a divergence in human motivation which is possibly amplified in the counterculture. In the case of the Collins brothers this is explained in part by their dysfunctional and unorthodox upbringing, with two powerful women bringing together contrasting determining influences:

> Their mother's madness, their orphaned state, their aunt's politics and their arbitrary identity formed in both a savage detachment for they found such detachment necessary to maintain their precarious autonomy'.[156]

Due to their socialist aunt's influence, the brothers set off in an abortive attempt to help the Cuban revolution while still children.[157] Buzz epitomises the outward trappings and lifestyle of the hippy culture since he wears crushed orange and purple clothes, smokes hashish, travels to north Africa and is drawn to the drama of socialist revolution. Such worldly ventures, however, do not seem to bring about his personal development or enhance his wisdom. Improbably, Carter explains Buzz as a character waiting for punk to happen in her later afterword for the novel.[158]

Three themes appear across Carter's Bristol trilogy, making them as O'Day argued 'circumstantial' and underscoring a sense of place. Several key characters experience discovery, excitement and find self-expression through the totemic power of things. While they live in a modern city they experience reality through the natural and human environment with its unique historical resonances. Finally, given the centrality of music in Carter's life, it should be of little surprise that a variety of musicians, musical influences and music venues appear throughout all three novels.

Both surrealist and situationist ideas influenced Angela Carter, informing her thinking and subtly conditioning her output. During the 1960s material prosperity enabled escalating capitalist consumerism in the West, increasingly

154 Carter, *Love*, 109-110. Annabel's solipsistic masochism is a counterpart to Honeybuzzard's sadism.
155 Carter, *Several Perceptions*, 6-7.
156 Carter, *Love*, 11.
157 Carter, *Love*, 14.
158 Carter's Afterword was added in 1987, *Love*, 116.

and more intensively determining the human relation to material objects. The radical counterculture began to question and challenge the role of the ownership of mass-produced consumer items in shaping status and identity and conveying social value. Indeed, capitalism's drive to place a resource, item or service's value upon the extent to which it could be commodified and realise a profit was a fundamental aspect of the dominant culture that the counterculture was against. Critic Max Blechman has described the Situationist International, at its peak in 1968, the year of the uprisings in Paris and across the world, as the 'pinnacle of the revolutionary avant-gardes of romanticism'.[159] The antipathy of the 1960s counterculture to the norms of capitalism place it firmly in the Romantic tradition, described by Karl Marx as the 'legitimate antithesis up to its blessed end'.[160] *Several Perceptions* and *Love* were written at a moment when surrealist and situationist ideas were directly influencing the counterculture. Joseph, the student and beatnik in *Several Perceptions*, has few personal possessions except a small collection of books, including one on Romantic-era poet William Blake and several on the Vietnam War.[161] The characters in *Love* are often acquisitive yet also have complicated perspectives and relationships to the common things around them. Carter even sometimes renders things themselves as characterful. For instance, there is a fabulous description of objects taking on the emotional patina of those who have owned them when Lee Collins returns home to find 'the tap dripped Annabel's tears and the very sofa seemed re-upholstered with her anguish'.[162] Unstimulated by the attractions of shopping, Annabel and Buzz also like to steal things, go to auctions and rake through the city tip. Their passion for objets trouvés recalls Morris's and Honeybuzzard's 'treasure hunting' exploits in *Shadow Dance*.

On a larger scale, the characters in Carter's Bristol trilogy inhabit a world of capitalist modernity, where their city is being physically reconfigured by new tower blocks and road schemes. Yet such momentous changes are rarely registered. Joseph, as we have seen, looks down on 'a flyover buzzing with traffic'[163] in *Several Perceptions*, while the solipsistic Annabel Collins takes note of several features including the 'skyscrapers of the city'[164] but these are merged into her own mindscape rather than having the substantial reality of

159 Max Blechman, 'Reflections on Revolutionary Romanticism', 237-250 in *Revolutionary Romanticism*, ed. by Max Blechman (San Francisco: City Lights, 1999), 246.
160 Blechman, quoting Marx's *Grundrisse* in 'Reflections on Revolutionary Romanticism', 237.
161 Carter, *Several Perceptions*, 14-15.
162 Carter, *Love*, 54.
163 Carter, *Several Perceptions*, 14.
164 Carter, *Love*. 2.

an urban landscape. In 1988 Carter reflected that 'Towards the end of the sixties it felt like living on a demolition site', which was true in the literal sense that she had seen with her own eyes the replacement of Victorian streets which were reduced to rubble to make way for vertical streets in the form of the new tower blocks of Lawrence Hill. It was the demolition and reconstruction of ideas, however, that was uppermost in her concerns. She continued that 'one felt one was living on the edge of the unimaginable; there was a constant sense of fear and excitement',[165] something that she attributed to the impact of global crises such as the Vietnam War on the social psyche. Her attitudes are conflicted and provisional, partly because of the immense diversity and complexity of change and its uncertain outcomes. Furthermore, the overarching ruptures between the traditional and the modern, and the establishment and the counterculture, were marked by countless conflicts within each.

This uncertainty is played out by the different depictions of the urban environment and responses among the characters that populate the novels that make up the Bristol trilogy. There is generally more fresh air in *Several Perceptions* and *Love* than there is in *Shadow Dance* where, for the most part, events unfold in pubs, cafes and shops, apart from some skulking in derelict houses and the local cemetery. In the brighter and more optimistic *Several Perceptions* outdoor scenes are for the most part in daylight, while in the edgier novel *Love* the action takes place in darker hours. While Annabel, Lee and Buzz are young, contemporary and urban, they also dwell in an interior universe often at radical variance with the reality surrounding them. The Bristol that is portrayed in *Love* is shot through by historical echoes and influences and the ambience of paranormal activity. For Annabel, suicide is preceded by experiences in which the quotidian is constantly transformed by twilight and the mundane destabilised by tricks of happenstance. From the outset, for example, she is profoundly unsettled by the apparent coincidence of the sunlight and 'absolute night' since the moon is visible at the same time which appals her as 'a dreadful rebellion of the familiar'.[166] Her delusions include a self-destructive version of the pathetic fallacy, at once looking up 'the district of terraces and crescents where she lived' (Clifton again) while attributing malignant agency to the natural world and believing herself 'at the whim of the roaring winds'. Excitement is indeed counterbalanced by fear. Elements of realism in the Bristol trilogy, therefore, are imaginatively refracted through the minds of characters who often have a tenuous hold upon the circumstances that surround them.

165 Carter, 'Truly, It Felt Like Year One', 211.
166 Carter, *Love*, 2-3.

Given the contextual importance of set and setting to Carter's early novels, I shall now turn to survey the counterculture that existed in Clifton in more detail. The latter chapters of this book consider both the nature of the Bohemian counterculture and its expression in the provincial domains of Bristol and Bath.

Scenes from Bohemian Clifton

There is a tendency to underplay, even to completely devalue, the experience of the 1960s, especially for women, but towards the end of that decade there was a brief period of public philosophical awareness that occurs only very occasionally in human history; when, truly, it felt like Year One, that all that was holy was in the process of being profaned and we were attempting to grapple with the real relations between human beings.[167]

Royal York Crescent and alternative Clifton

From 1961 to 1969, Angela and Paul Carter's address was the Ground Floor Flat, 38 Royal York Crescent in the heart of Clifton.[168] The Clifton and Hotwells Improvement Society has not, so far, seen fit to mark Angela Carter's residence with one of their dark green memorial plaques to noteworthy or interesting people who lived in the district. This is ironic, given that, together with Christopher Frayling, she unsuccessfully made a bid for Mary Shelley's achievement as an internationally renowned novelist to be recognised with a plaque in Bath.[169] One of the great architectural landmarks of Bristol, and one of the longest structures of its kind in Europe, the character of Royal York Crescent has shifted since its construction between 1791 and 1820. Improbably from the perspective of the present day, the vast Royal York Crescent was the centre of Clifton's bohemian society. The photograph of this elegantly turned

167 Angela Carter, 'Notes from the Front Line' [1983], 36-43 in *Shaking a Leg: Journalism and Writings*, ed. by Jenny Uglow (London: Vintage, 1998), 37, with reference to Karl Marx's *Communist Manifesto*.

168 And, very briefly, in 1969, on the 5th Floor of 27 Royal York Crescent. Gordon, *Invention of Angela Carter*, 133.

169 Frayling, Inside the Bloody Chamber, 15-16. The author of Frankenstein certainly deserved the tribute and Carter and Frayling also felt it necessary to address the under-representation of the achievements of women writers. Frayling finally achieved his ambition to unveil a plaque to Mary Shelley in Bath in 2018: Maev Kennedy, '"A 200-Year-Old Secret": Plaque to Mark Bath's Hidden Role in Frankenstein', The Guardian (26 February 2018): https://www.theguardian.com/books/2018/feb/26/a-200-year-old-secret-plaque-to-mark-baths-hidden-role-in-frankenstein [accessed 23 November 2018].

Clifton's Royal York Crescent (1962).

construction, foregrounded with a single person and dog, was taken in 1962, the year after Angela and Paul Carter moved in. From the delicious light and shadows, they appear to be walking westwards illuminated by the evening sun.

A journal entry for 3rd January, written when Angela Carter was 22, evocatively captures the same scene in the bitter winter of 1963:

> Still snow, deep. There are little passages like rabbit tracks, cut along the Crescent & people tread along them delicate as cats. Snow caked on hair, hats, shoulders of people in the street as in cartoons. Georgian Clifton looks beautiful, like a black & white engraving, every ledge & railing thickly topped, whipped cream spread prodigally.[170]

Dave Lawton remembered that a social visit while the Carters were living at Royal York Crescent would be a special occasion, although totally informal and an opportunity for a laugh:

> Me and Sue [his partner of the time] we'd go round for dinner. She loved waiter, waiter jokes. She made a super cheesecake. I remember when she came round to us we'd see her coming and make fun of her

170 British Library Archive: Angela Carter Papers: Journal Add. Ms88899/1/88: 1962-1963?. Bob Baker also particularly recalled this ruthlessly harsh winter, when he was frozen in for three months while living at West Mall with his family, which included three very young children. Bob Baker, Skype interview with the author (24 January 2019).

because she had a big grey leather handbag, a foot by a foot, which we used to call Angela's 'elephant scrotum' handbag. But she didn't mind. She was full of humour you know.[171]

Bob Gale also often called in at the Carters' Royal York Crescent flat during the early 1960s after striking up a friendship with Paul Carter, due to their connections through the folk scene. He soon came to know Angela as well and was grateful for her kindness during a prolonged illness when she would visit and make him cheese on toast in his flat in the neighbouring Goldney Road. He recalled that 'When I first met Angela she was really obsessed about making bread' which she was baking using a recipe from an early edition of Mrs Beeton. 'I was actually the first person to taste her bread—it tasted awful, but she did get much better'. Gale was able to provide a closely observed description of the Carters' flat in an interview:

> They lived in the ground floor flat. There was the hall. There was a very, very large room. The main sitting room. Looking across the room there was an Evans fireplace which was quite fine because the building was built around 1800. There was a comfortable sofa, a rocking chair which Angela had bought, and she used to sit in. It was very moderately furnished. There was one painting on the wall which was by Peter Swan. I thought it was terrible. I didn't like it. Angela said when you can do better let me know. There were steps to the kitchen on the left. There were two rooms at the back which were the study and bedroom. There was a rather fine mirror over the fireplace.[172]

While it was being built, the Crescent was a precarious commercial venture, taking nearly three decades to complete after its commencement in 1791. Nonetheless, it remains a testament to the art of designing high-density housing that is durable and desirable. As recollections from those who lived in the Crescent show, by the 1960s the well-to-do residents had long since been ousted. A new generation of creative workers and students had replaced them and, notwithstanding the spartan conditions, were enjoying the opportunity to live with spacious rooms and stunning views. At that time, it seems that much good use of the space was made. Royal York Crescent and

171 Dave Lawton, telephone interview with the author (18 January 2018). Another of Angela Carter's 'Waiter, waiter…' jokes is served up at the end of the text.
172 Bob Gale, telephone interview with the author (26 November 2018). Carter namechecks Mrs Beeton in *Shadow Dance*, 88.

the adjacent crescents and terraces were a hive of activity, their individual cells filling with the honey of cultural endeavour to enjoy hedonistically in the 'festal' atmosphere of the era. Arguably, the creative energy of the crescent dwellers was to be recycled, with its momentum ongoing in the following years and decades when Bristol's reputation as an imaginative, diverse and radical city was consolidated. This beneficial effect was felt long after Clifton had regentrified and the creative impetus had swarmed to other suburbs and neighbourhoods.

The script-writer, Bob Baker, experienced life in 1960s Clifton as empowering and energising. Brought-up in in the suburb of St George to the east of the city, Baker began the 1960s working as a stone mason employed by the Co-op. His output speeded up when he shifted from hammer and chisel to typewriter as he became a professional writer. Early collaborations found him working on *Some People*, Clive Donner's 1962 feature film about the seminal Bristol music scene, and with film director John Boorman, who worked for the BBC in Bristol during the early 1960s making documentaries such as *The Newcomers*, featuring Bristol writer A. C. H. Smith, Alison Smith and playwright Tom Stoppard. Baker found that the combination of social creativity and affordability made Clifton a place of possibilities and opportunities:

> There was an air of almost repressed art, people that desperately wanted to do things but hadn't thought they could do it, somehow the 60s let them free. The Beatles were the example of the dawning of the greatness of the working-class grammar school boy, they had the grounding in working-class but then had the imagination to take it further and I felt I was one of those. I'd gone to a secondary modern school.

> If you had an idea you could pursue it. You couldn't have done it in the '50s. There would have been so many ways to stop you doing it, having good fun. Old farts would say you can't do that because of dodiddlydiddlydee… You felt subversive doing anything for quite a while.

> I'd bought an old house, and for example, there were three writers just on Windsor Terrace out of ten houses, so that's not bad going… There was a sense of an energy about and I just forged ahead and did things and I didn't think about them. I always wanted to make films and so I built a rostrum in my basement and I suddenly found that

people were desperate to make their own films and so they came to me, so I got involved in making other people's films. And, so, I'd done up this wreck that I'd bought for 45 quid, and it was an ever-open shop.

There was a genuine feeling that every year was summer, it was great, it was fun.[173]

The interface between the University and the creative community was also productive. When Baker and co-writer Dave Martin needed to check out scientific details for *Dr Who*, such as how long someone could survive in a sealed room or the physics of time-travel, they could check the logistical possibilities with Dave Lawton at the Physics Department. Lawton was happy for his advice to be repaid in cider.[174]

By the 1960s, the formerly well-to-do late Georgian and Regency Royal York Crescent was at the heart of Clifton's thriving alternative culture, with its plentiful low-cost flats; today it is again, for the most part, the preserve of millionaires. Carter places the events in *Several Perceptions* in 'a once-handsome, now decayed district' inhabited mostly by old people, students and 'beatniks who nested in attics',[175] a description entirely in keeping with accounts of people who lived in Clifton at the time. Former resident Ed Newsom described his experience of living in a Royal York Crescent flat during the late 1960s:

It was unfurnished, bitterly cold, no central heating, just a gas fire in one room, but it was very cheap. [...] The other thing I remember about it when I lived there was that the Suspension Bridge end of Royal York Crescent was really quite derelict, it wasn't in a very good state at all.[176]

Another interviewee, Bob Gale, corroborated this state of widespread dilapidation:

Clifton was a slum until gentrification started in 1973. You could go along Cornwallis Crescent and all the facing would be falling off the

173 Bob Baker, Skype interview with the author (24 January 2019). The other writers in Windsor Terrace were Angela Rodaway and Ivan Benbrook.
174 Bob Baker, Skype interview with the author (24 January 2019); Dave Lawton, telephone interview with the author (1 January 2019).
175 Carter, *Several Perceptions*, 9.
176 Ed Newsom and Al Read, interview with the author (M Shed, Bristol 8 August 2018).

houses. Most of the basements of Royal York Crescent were empty and people used to raid them for stuff and took what they wanted.[177]

There were positive consequences of ungentrification. Gale realised that the low rents were a great asset to artists like himself: 'Clifton was very affordable at the time. I was paying 32/6 [£1.62½]. There was a buzz'.[178] As we shall see, for those musicians, writers and artists willing to put up with discomfort, a district with a low cost of living and minimum rent represented a great opportunity. Speaking of inner-city Manchester, Roger Hutchinson put the matter nicely in *Oz* when he said that dereliction and demolition sites 'mean minimal rent for an indeterminate number of months. And minimum rent, as sure eggs is eggs, means freaks'.[179] Al Read, who also lived in Clifton during the 1960s and 1970s, mentioned the role of rent controls in place at the time as an important factor too, making it difficult for landlords to charge exorbitant rents or evict tenants in the rented sector.[180]

Creative workers and students were able to turn low rent to good account. Like Newsom, Ian A. Anderson recalls:

Royal York Crescent in those days was run down, tatty and bohemian. The flats I knew were all cold and damp (no central heating back then) and cheap to rent, so there were plenty of students, artists, musicians, writers etc. The courtyard/basement flat at 12a was handed on through several years of University folk club organisers, and I ended up taking it over in 1969 through to 1973 when I moved out of Bristol. We started and ran our Village Thing label from there in 1970 and several albums were recorded in the living room. Good acoustics![181]

The opportunities this situation presented diminished from the late 1960s onwards, as housing stock became less affordable, and the built environment became increasingly contested territory. Local enterprise bids to capitalise at the expense of Bristol's historical and architectural heritage and natural environment, bolstered by council policy, met with community resistance in Clifton and across the city. Now largely mainstream, campaigns to protect and enhance the city's natural and urban environment and architectural assets had

177 Bob Gale, telephone interview with the author (26 November 2018).
178 Bob Gale, telephone interview with the author (26 November 2018).
179 Roger Hutchinson, 'Sledgehammers in the Slums!', *Oz* 42 (May/June 1972), 37.
180 Ed Newsom and Al Read, interview with the author (M Shed, Bristol 8 August 2018).
181 Ian A. Anderson, e-mail to the author (2 July 2018).

The Bristol Troubadour gang, Royal York Crescent, 1970. Left to right: Lee, Andy Leggett (of Pigsty Hill Light Orchestra), Janet, Tim Hodgson (then Bristol Troubadour manager), Jane, Ian Turner (a.k.a. 'Heavy Drummer'), Eve, Maggie Holland, Ian A Anderson, Pat Roche, Ian Hunt.

their roots in the late 1960s and 1970s counterculture.[182] The tale of the loss of historic buildings in Bristol since the Second World War is a melancholy one, and homes, public houses, schools and chapels of architectural interest continue to be demolished.[183] Opposition to the destruction, however, has also marked up some notable successes. Both the defeats and victories of the 1960s and 1970s are retold in detail in Gordon Priest and Pamela Cobb's *The Fight for Bristol* (1980). The high-profile battles against the Bristol

182 The history of the city's ecological movement is recorded in Emmelie Brownlee, *Bristol's Green Roots: The Growth of the Environmental Movement in the City of Bristol* (Bristol: Schumacher Centre, 2011)

183 In my own area of east Bristol, for example, both the city's first Primitive Methodist Chapel, the Ebenezer Chapel in St Philip's built around 1849, and the late nineteenth-century Board School in Avonvale Road, Redfield were demolished in 2014 despite local opposition. The historic White Hart in Whitehall shared their fate in 2018, after it was designated an 'exciting development opportunity' following its closured in 2015. East Bristol lacks the conservation area protection afforded to other districts of the city, such as Clifton.

Development Plan and against proposals to build a huge hotel and car park complex in the Avon Gorge, in particular, had consequences for Clifton and the surrounding wards. From the early 1970s onwards, the ecology movement also began to blossom in the Clifton area. Bristol's present-day reputation as an environmentally friendly city largely dates from the efforts of campaigners and activists of the 1960s and 1970s.

In 1966 a coalition of concerned citizens and local groups emerged to oppose the Bristol Development Plan, which set out proposals for a huge Outer Circuit Road which began to fundamentally reconfigure the spatial geography of the city. Early stages of the road cleft apart communities and destroyed areas of Easton and Totterdown in particular. Architect and campaigner George Ferguson (later mayor) recorded that plans for the road would 'tear up the side of Brandon Hill, dive into the hillside and underneath Clifton… reappear behind the Victoria Rooms with a great spaghetti junction, go up to Tyndall's Park… tearing through houses… [and then] dive down through Cotham into St Paul's…'[184]

To date, published accounts of the 1960s 'underground' have tended to focus upon alternative society in the capital, rather than chronicling the history of the provincial English, Welsh and Scottish counterculture.[185] The underground scene in London may have magnetically attracted kindred spirits from all over,

The 'plant a tree' initiative was promoted by the Bristol Visual and Environmental Group for future generations.

and its force field came to be felt across the world, but it was a resolutely metropolitan affair. Leading first-hand accounts, such as Jeff Nuttall's *Bomb Culture* (1968), Richard Neville's *Play Power* (1970), Jonathan Green's, *Days in the Life: Voices from the English Underground, 1961–1971* (1990), Roger Hutchinson's *High Sixties* (1992), Mick Farren's *Give the Anarchist a Cigarette* (2001), Joe Boyd's *White Bicycles* (2006), Miles' *London Calling* (2010) all enticingly capture the zeitgeist but rarely concern themselves with happenings west of Ealing or north of Enfield. Many of those that wished to 'make it' from the West Country, such as Bristolian prog

184 Brownlee, *Bristol's Green Roots*, 41.
185 Rob Young's encyclopaedic *Electric Eden: Unearthing Britain's Visionary Music* (2010), however, travels the regions on a wonderful journey through the underground music of the 1960s and 1970s and much more besides.

rockers East of Eden, swiftly headed eastwards beyond Swindon to try their luck in the capital. But what was going on elsewhere among the hazy groves and in the patchouli-sweetened garrets of Albion?

Outside of London, it has been suggested that Bristol and Canterbury had the most prominent and highly developed countercultural scenes during the late 1960s.[186] By the mid-1970s, Bath was also a notable stronghold for the alternative society, with Nicholas Saunders writing in 1975 that the West Country 'doesn't have an exceptional number of freak settlers except in Bath'.[187] The remaining chapters look at some countercultural expressions from the world of music, literature and alternative performance and dissident voices emanating from Angela Carter's Clifton and the surrounding wards, across Bristol, into the West Country and beyond. Folk, jazz, prog rock and psychedelia were pumping out from the Georgian buildings, students occupied Bristol University, early St Paul's Carnivals and free festivals were staged, craft artists such as toy designer Ron Fuller were working in Royal York Crescent and in workshops and studios across the district, feminists in Redland and Cotham were at the forefront of the emerging women's liberation movement, experimental art, writing and theatre was inspired by—and in some cases inspiring—international developments, buildings were squatted while housing activists made life difficult for property speculators and profiteering landlords, cannabis joints were rolled and LSD trips undertaken, the Bristol Dwarfs and ecologists were imagining alternative societies. Half a century later, the Bristol Radical History Festival held at the M Shed in May 2018 revisited the events of 1968 in the city. This survey intends to continue this process by capturing more fading, forgotten and hidden histories through the recollections of those that were there and other primary sources.

Clifton Electric: The rock music scene

The burgeoning counterculture in Bristol ensured that it was on the national and international circuit for the top acts in the rock revolution, including The Beatles, The Rolling Stones, The Who, Jimi Hendrix Experience, Pink Floyd, The Yardbirds and Bob Dylan. Thrilling and appalling the critics, Dylan treated the West Country to a blast of his mid-west genius at the height of the controversy over his switch to electric guitar. Angela Carter enthusiastically reviewed Dylan's performance at Cardiff in 1966, being fully behind his transformation to what she termed 'the first all-electronic, all existential rock

186 John Row, personal conversation with the author, 15 September 2018 (Swindon).
187 Nicholas Saunders *et al.*, *Alternative England and Wales* (London: Nicholas Saunders, 1975), 16.

and roll singer'. She revelled in his creation of a stylised persona and the lyricism of songs which displayed 'a mature savagery and a scary kind of wit which is new and extraordinary in music of mass appeal'.[188] Dylan's appearance in Bristol on the same tour made for a highly memorable encounter for Gary Hicks, Carter's collaborator on the Bristol student *Nonesuch* magazine:

> When Bob Dylan played the Colston Hall on 10th May 1966 Michael Kullman [friend and writer who put on experimental plays] got me into Dylan's suite in the Grand Hotel, Bristol afterwards where the icon was holding court to about half a dozen followers. We stayed until 5am and helped fight off an attempt by the Bristol University rugby team to rough up Dylan—by putting some furniture against the door. They banged on it for a while and then went off.
>
> Stupidly, Kullman accused Dylan of going commercial with the electric guitar and Dylan responded by saying 'You are the kind of guy who farts on his mother's cushions after Sunday lunch', i.e. accusing him of being a kind of pseudo beatnik.
>
> Dylan strumming his guitar was very funny, with an acid tongue, throughout saying things like 'Your queen is just a Kentucky chick with her stilted way of speaking'.[189]

Sleeve cover for Ian A. Anderson's Royal York Crescent (1970).

But now let us turn to the home-grown talent of this period. In Bristol, the crescents and terraces of Clifton nurtured the most abundant creativity in music, art, literature and the performing arts during the 1960s. Ian A. Anderson modestly didn't mention that his own acoustic folk album called *Royal York Crescent,* released in 1970, and several others were among the output of The Village Thing and Saydisc record labels of this time.[190] Prominent among the musicians that recorded on The Village Thing label at Royal York Crescent

188 Quotes from Angela Carter, 'Bob Dylan on Tour', [1966], 323-325 in Uglow (ed.), *Shaking a Leg*, 324.
189 Gary Hicks, e-mail to the author (4 January 2019).
190 Mark Jones suggests that Anderson distanced himself from his Village Thing albums during the later 1970s in *Bristol Folk*, 28.

were Fred Wedlock and the Pigsty Hill Light Orchestra, something of a house band for the Troubadour Club.[191] Bristol-bred folk singer Fred Wedlock, famous for the unlikely comic hit 'The Oldest Swinger in Town', experienced the city's creative diversity and vitality as a far younger swinger, performing regularly from the late 1960s onwards. With their motley collection of orthodox and home-made instruments, former Troubadour Club regular John Waller recalled that The Pigsty Hill Light Orchestra:

> ...were brilliant. Crammed onto this tiny stage they would crash through a series of anarchic jazz/folk/blues/trad/I don't know what numbers; in a way that defied description. It was theatre as much as music. They did release a record (called Phlop) but it barely hints at the delights of their stage performance.[192]

Anderson still enjoys the irony that it was the Clifton folkies of the late 1960s that first popularised the appellation of Clifton Village:

> It was us lot who hung out around the corner at the Troubadour club in Waterloo Street (and Splinters coffee house) who invented and first started using the address Clifton Village—now acknowledged on a blue plaque—because we were thinking of the then-recent Greenwich Village folk scene in New York.[193]

Al Stewart's 'Clifton in the Rain', released on his first album 'Bedsitter Images' (1967) and performed at the Troubadour Club, was the most celebrated song to capture the vibe of Clifton Village at this time:

> The listeners in the Troubadour
> Guitar player weaves a willow strain
> I took my love to Clifton in the rain

Local author Mike Jones records that when the Troubadour closed in 1971 the Village Thing linked up with Plastic Dog, which had become the leading agency for promoting Bristol's independent music scene from the late 1960s onwards. At this time, Plastic Dog was based at the Granary Club,

191 Jones, *Bristol Folk*, 80.
192 John Waller, 'Memories of the Bristol Troubadour': http://www.nawaller.com/wol/troubadour.html [accessed 9 August 2018].
193 Ian A. Anderson, e-mail to the author (2 July 2018). Perhaps also an ironic reference to the Village which forms the setting for *The Prisoner,* the TV series which acquired cult status on its release in 1967-68?

founded off the Welsh Back in 1968, which had emerged as a major venue for rock and acid-folk and which continued to host alternative music until its closure twenty years later in 1988. Founder members of The Granary, Al Read and Ed Newsom, were also at the heart of the Clifton music scene. Ed Newsom lived three doors down from Ian A. Anderson in the Ground Floor Flat at 9 Royal York Crescent from around 1968 to 1970. Another neighbour was Keith Wilkins who produced the 'amazing light shows' that were so much a part of the Granary experience in the early years.[194] One of the most memorable nights recalled by Newsom and Read was a performance by the Mothers of Invention, after which the band members were invited to come back to Royal York Crescent for a party.[195]

Al Read started with an early skiffle band during the late 1950s, managed rock nights at The Granary Club from 1968 to 1988, was a long-running BBC Bristol radio presenter and contributed to the major M Shed exhibition 'Bristol Music: Seven Decades of Sound' held in 2018. He was a huge help in writing this book and continued to support the Bristol music scene to the end of his life in 2019.

West Mall, Clifton, where Stackridge, Al Read of East of Eden and Flash Gordon were once tenants.

Read lived at addresses in West Mall and Vyvyan Terrace during the late 1950s and 1960s. He found that musicians were in demand at this time since DJs had not really become established and bands were often invited to play live at house parties and other functions. The solstitial party that concludes Carter's *Several Perceptions* features an invented band called 'Electric Opera', who are no doubt based upon one of the Clifton bands of

194 Remembering Wilkins' contribution to the Granary Club, Newsom also recalled that Wilkins was later to become a world champion yachtsman. Ed Newsom and Al Read, interview with the author (M Shed, Bristol 8 August 2018).
195 Ed Newsom and Al Read recalled a band member trying to open a wine bottle by repeatedly banging it against the wall, adding to the patina of alcohol and cigarette ash on what turned out to be an extremely valuable antique Persian carpet, interview with the author (M Shed, Bristol 8 August 2018).

the era, illustrating the way that the presence of live music could transform a house gathering into a memorable event. During the mid-1960s Read played with the bands Alan G. Read and The Statesmen and Franklyn Big Six. The latter became established on the Bristol circuit, supporting visits by major bands including Cream, when they played at the new Students' Union building, and The Hollies.[196]

It is as lead vocalist for the early East of Eden that Read has a more enduring place in rock history, since they were a significant prog rock band with their origins in Bristol in 1967.[197] The early, Bristol-based East of Eden played venues in Clifton such as the University's Victoria Rooms and even the huge former ballroom beneath the Grand Spa Hotel. Outside of the city, Read remembers playing in venues in the capital such as The Marquee and Eel Pie Island on the Thames, sharing billings in a support capacity with the likes of The Crazy World of Arthur Brown, Jethro Tull and The Nice. A particularly memorable highlight was the invitation to appear in Tony Richardson's film *Laughter in the Dark* in 1968. Bands such as Pink Floyd and The Nice had been considered but were unavailable, so East of Eden were pleased to step in. Their involvement was to perform live as entertainment for a three-day party at a large house in Hampstead. Read recalled that there was plenty of champagne available but less food. Events came to a head for the early East of Eden line-up after a gig on the Isle of Wight (not the festival), was followed by ongoing arguments on the return trip. Beyond personal disputes, there were differences about the direction the band was taking musically. Read admired David Arbus as a guitarist but disliked the direction the band was taking, with its recently adopted jazz base and lyrical content that he felt lacked meaning. Read, Terry Brace and Tony Fennell all split from the band shortly afterwards.[198] Read outlined why the Bristol part of the band split during the late 1960s:

> East of Eden did really well, you know. We nearly made it. Very close. It was only because we had our total differences and just didn't see eye to eye on anything. In fact, we split in half. So, bass, drums and guitar—which was me—and the three of us we all left at the same time. And we thought they were going the wrong way.[199]

196 Bob Baker, Skype interview with the author (24 January 2019).
197 Their first gig was at The Bamboo Club, St Pauls, in 1967. East of Eden official website: http://www.eastofedentheband.co.uk/index.html [accessed 5 August 2018].
198 Details in this paragraph from Al Read, personal conversation with the author at Granary Club 50th anniversary night (Golden Lion, Bishopston, Bristol, 30 December 2018).
199 Ed Newsom and Al Read, interview with the author (M Shed, Bristol 8 August 2018).

East of Eden moved to London and continued with a substantially different line-up, while the musicians in Bristol played as Barnaby Goode.

Clifton was likewise the original home of Stackridge who went on to achieve national renown. Stackridge emerged from Griptight Thynne who had shared the billing with Barnaby Goode at The Granary Club. They held their first rehearsals in Royal York Crescent in 1969; founder member and guitarist Andy Davis also lived in Ed Newsom's flat in the Crescent. Stackridge have since attracted attention as the band that opened at the small, informal and low budget gathering at Michael Eavis's Worthy Farm, called Pilton Pop, Blues and Folk Festival, in September 1970. This event was, of course, the origin of Glastonbury Festival. 1970 found band members living at 32 West Mall, Clifton, an address that was to be memorably captured in the song of that title. The opening lines of '32 West Mall' show that gentrification had some way to go at this date:

> A telegram arrived, the rent was overdue
> It's good to be alive, although the roof was leaking too
> Forty missing floorboards, fifty frantic "far out" mice below

Magic Muscle were another long-running band with Clifton roots (with a contact address at 2 Royal York Crescent) who also started in 1969. Magic Muscle represent a closer connection between Bristol and the underground 'scene' in London, given their links and shared personnel with the Pink Fairies, Crazy World of Arthur Brown, the Third Ear Band and, above all, Hawkwind. They were a loose collective of musicians that played raw but tight psychedelic free-form rock and supported Hawkwind with such regularity that they became known as 'The Bastard Sons of Hawkwind'. Band members were living in a commune variously known as 'Fun House' or 'Freaks' Castle' at 49 Cotham Brow by the early 1970s.[200] Renting the basement, Magic Muscle members were at the core of Bristol bohemia, linked to the anarchistic Dwarf Party, the local chapter of the Hells Angels and the Bristol Free Festival held on Clifton Downs in 1971. Magic Muscle formed a nexus that indicates how close-knit the 1960s and 1970s Clifton counterculture had become.[201]

The address at 49 Cotham Brow, moreover, connects us closely to Angela Carter's circle. The building was bought at auction in 1963 and jointly-owned by the Orsborn and Thorne families until the latter moved out in the later

---

200 Gill Loats and John Sprinks, *Bristol Boys Make More Noise!: The Bristol Music Scene 1974-1981* (Bristol: Tangent, 2014), 9 and 58.

201 Magic Muscle had various line-ups and several reunions over the years, eventually merging into Brevis Frond, a band which continues in the present day.

Annabel Rees (née Lawson), Jeremy Rees and John Orsborn, at the opening of the Arnolfini in March 1961. (courtesy of Arnolfini and Bristol Archives).

1960s.[202] According to a blog by Pat and Dave Thorne's nephew Nick Gilbert, the Orsborns lived in the upper part of the premises and rented out the rest to multiple occupants who worked together as musicians and activists, thus giving the building a communal vibe.[203] In 1961 John and Jenny Orsborn had collaborated with Jeremy Rees and Annabel Lawson, as initial funders and founder members of what was to become the Arnolfini art gallery, originally based in Triangle West in Clifton.[204] The photograph below shows three of the founders in front of a painting by Peter Swan. [205] Gordon tells us that Angela Carter first met John and Jenny Orsborn during the early 1960s when they

202 The Thorne family moved out in 1966-67. Pat Thorne, e-mail to Nick Gilbert (8 December 2018).
203 Nick Gilbert, 'Every Album I Own: M is for Magic Muscle': https://planktonproduktions. wordpress.com/2017/12/20/every-album-i-own-m-is-for-magic-muscle/ (20 December 2017) [accessed 13 August 2018].
204 Mel Gooding, '[Obituary of] Jeremy Rees: Visionary Administrator who Built a Thriving Arts Centre in the West Country', *The Guardian* (20 December 2003): https://www. theguardian.com/news/2003/dec/20/guardianobituaries.artsobituaries [online] [accessed 13 August 2018] and Mary Ackland, 'Arnolfini: The Honeymoon Years', 54-58 in *The 60s in Bristol*, ed. by James Belsey (Bristol: Redcliffe, 1989), 55-56. Another good friend of Angela Carter during the 1960s, Nick Gray, also mentioned a contribution to the Arnolfini 'Our claim to fame in the Bristol art world was moving the Arnolfini Gallery from one side of the docks to the other by boat when Jeremy [Rees] opened Bush House', Nick Gray, e-mail to the author (5 June 2018)
205 Phil Owen, e-mail to the author (19 February 2019). See Phil Owen, 'Enjoy Yourself: An Introduction to Arnolfini's History', Arnolfini blog: https://www.arnolfini.org.uk/blog/enjoy-yourself. [accessed 29 December 2018].

lived at Saville Place, immediately adjacent to Royal York Crescent, and became drinking companions at the Greyhound pub on Princess Victoria Street. Carter had loosely taken John Orsborn as the model for Honeybuzzard, in many ways the chief, and in all ways the most nefarious, character in her first novel *Shadow Dance*. John Orsborn's status as the prototype for Honeybuzzard was based not only on the fact that he was an artist who never quite became professional, and that he salvaged bric-à-brac from derelict buildings, but was also in Gordon's depiction (based on accounts of those who knew him) a charismatic man but whose 'attributes' included philandering and manipulation.[206] Angela Carter had an affair with John Orsborn in 1966-1967,[207] after the publication of *Shadow Dance*, thereby ironically falling for the partial image of her own detested creation.

Several commentators report that the address at Cotham Brow was to become notorious, especially when Magic Muscle were in residence after 1969:

Clenched fist fretboard image from Bristol Voice (August 1976).

> Out of this wild, semi-communal scene, in which the great and good of Bristol bohemia—artists and antique dealers, academics. poets and jazz heads—would mingle with the counter-culture, jamming, painting, tripping (above all tripping) Magic Muscle didn't so much spring as slowly, organically coalesce.[208]

Adrian Shaw, Magic Muscle's bass player, even goes so far to claim that at this time band members 'took acid virtually every day for some while and certainly for every gig we played'.[209] This raises the question of whether Angela Carter dropped acid while in Bristol? While Carter was connected to this circle through Orsborn, their affair was over before the advent of Magic

206 Gordon, *Invention of Angela Carter*, 60-61; 79-80.
207 Gordon, *Invention of Angela Carter*, 112.
208 Gilbert, 'Every Album I Own'.
209 Shaw interview, 'Dislike of Authority and Barbers…'

Muscle. I have found no evidence that she was inspired by LSD or had any other mind-altering drug experiences during her years in Bristol, despite the hallucinatory quality of some of her fiction. Indeed, the evidence of three friends who knew her in the West Country in the 1960s and 1970s is that she did not partake. Curry corroborates that such drugs were not a part of their lives while at the University of Bristol and that there was 'No drug scene. There were "purple hearts" around during finals—either to calm us down or provide mental energy, can't remember which and probably did neither'.[210] Frayling shares an anecdote that a mathematics lecturer once asked Edward Horesh, in reference to Carter's role, 'who is teaching them all to smoke pot?', but believes that this was 'Very unlikely actually, but he may have been speaking metaphorically'.[211] More specifically linked to her association with John Orsborn and his connection to Magic Muscle, Dave Lawton knew of the commune at Cotham as a source of acid and remembered members of the band with their 'Muscle bus' but said that, as far as he knew, Angela Carter was familiar with the local beatnik and bohemian scene but did not get involved with the Bristol acid culture of the late 1960s and early 1970s, by which time she had left for London.[212]

'Rustic' Rod Goodway has wonderfully recounted the story of the commune at Cotham, recalling the time when he lived in the large rambling building from 1969 to the early 1970s with fellow members of Magic Muscle, Keith Christmas and others.[213] Into this scene quickly arrived the Bristol West Coast chapter of the Hells Angels. Adrian Shaw later suggested that the Hells Angels bonded with them because 'We shared a dislike of authority and barbers and a love of music and drugs'.[214] As we shall see, Magic Muscle became politically active in a countercultural way.

210 Neil Curry, e-mail to the author (5 October 2018).

211 Frayling, *Inside the Bloody Chamber*, 18.

212 Dave Lawton, telephone interview with the author (16 September 2018).

213 *It's Psychedelic Baby!* magazine, 'Interview with "Space Rocker" Rustic Rod Goodway about Magic Muscle...' http://www.psychedelicbabymag.com/2017/04/interview-with-space-rocker-rustic-rod.html [online] [accessed 19 August 2018]; Aching Cellar website, ''Magic Muscle': http://www.achingcellar.co.uk/pages/tree/magic_muscle.htm [accessed 19 August 2018].

214 Heart of the Sea Blog, ''A Dislike of Authority and Barbers and a Love of Music and Drugs': An Interview with Adrian Shaw': http://zhou520.blogspot.com/2008/09/dislike-of-authority-and-barbers-and.html [accessed 28 December 2018].

Writerly Clifton: Literature and performance

My God, there was some talent around Bristol! Not just musicians, writers and singers but painters, poets and actors too—all cheerfully borrowing from each other and building up their own acts (Fred Wedlock).[215]

Angela Carter's work as a poet has often been overlooked. However, poetry contributed to both her development as a writer and to her immersion in literary culture during her time in Bristol. Her published collection *Unicorn* covers the years 1963-1971, a period that largely overlaps with her residence in Royal York Crescent. Historian Rosemary Hill, who compiled the collection of Carter's verses republished in 2015, records that the first edition was co-edited with Neil Curry from 112 Redland Road, Bristol. The original is now extremely rare; Hill beautifully describes the battered copy held in the British Library as looking like 'a scruffy guest announced by a suave butler'.[216] With her early interest in the Beats, Angela Carter was situated on the fringes of the British Poetry Revival, with Bristol University being a regional hub. Together Carter and Curry edited a local poetry magazine called *Vision* at the University in 1963 and the latter records that they 'ran the Literary Society and invited safe speakers: RS Thomas who didn't reply, Vernon Watkins came and was splendid'.[217] The Welsh poet Vernon Watkins would have been warmly welcomed and of great interest, both as Dylan Thomas's close friend and as a significant writer in his own right.

Poetry was a rich source of inspiration for Carter's experimental writing which was created by sending taproots down into both medieval tales and ballads and modernist verse. In her best work, she attained an inimitable synthesis of the two, expressed through the vivid imagery of her fiction, with its combination of the arcane, the exotic and quixotic episodes of the commonplace.

Carter was among many writers and artists in Clifton attracted to the University of Bristol and the nearby Royal West of England Academy and who developed a synergistic relationship with the surrounding community and the alternative 'scene'. The collective quills of the local poets caused several journals and anthologies to take flight during the 1960s. The widely published

---

215 Jones, *Bristol Folk,* 163.
216 Rosemary Hill, 'A Splinter in the Mind: The Poems of Angela Carter', essay in *Unicorn: The Poetry of Angela Carter* (London: Profile, 2015), 50. The republication of Carter's poetry was undertaken by Rosemary Hill in memory of her late husband, the poet Christopher Logue who had met Angela twice in Bristol during the 1960s and admired her as a poet.
217 Neil Curry, e-mail to the author (5 October 2018).

Cardiff-born poet John James (1939-2018) contributed the locally-coloured 'Bathampton Morrismen at the Rose & Crown' to the classic collection of alternative poetry *Children of Albion: Poetry of the Underground in Britain* (1969) and includes tributes to Bristol creative artists in his work 'October 27 1969: For Barry Flanagan' and 'Song after Richard Long and Johnny Cash'. A communist earlier in his career, James moved to Bristol around 1960 to begin a degree course at the University. He supported his studies by taking on several night jobs, including working as a dance hall bouncer.[218] In the early 1960s, he established a friendship with sculptor Barry Flanagan while they worked night-shifts in Parker's Bakery in Cotham, apparently finding poetic and artistic metaphors in the jam doughnuts that they processed.[219] James came to know poets Nick Wayte and Chris Torrance while studying at the University and lived in the city until 1966. John James and Nick Wayte began *The Resuscitator* in 1963, an avant-garde journal of poetry and literature, the first issues of which were published in Bristol by View Publications.[220] Little additional biographical information is known about Nick Wayte (N.R. Wayte), a poet and lecturer from Cheltenham who socialised with both John James and Barry Flanagan in Bristol and who was also a contributor to *The English Intelligencer* and *Move*. The poetry of John James and Chris Torrance also appeared in the late 1960s *English Intelligencer*, which was particularly influential in the British Poetry Revival.

Cover of Nick Wayte's 1969 poetry collection, *Seconds*.

Chris Torrance lived in Bristol from 1966 to 1970. While working as a Park Department labourer, he contributed to *The Resuscitator* and, like James, to Michael Horowitz's *Children of Albion* anthology as well as producing his early collections, *Green Orange Purple Red* (1968) and *Aries Under Saturn and Beyond* (1969).[221]

218 Nicholas Johnson, 'John James Obituary', *The Guardian* (29 June 2018) [online] [accessed 25 July 2018].

219 Interview with John James in Peter Bach, *The Man Who Sculpted Hares—Barry Flanagan, A Life* (Broadcast BBC4 9 October 2012): https://vimeo.com/111528057

220 Angela Carter was familiar with the *Resuscitator*, noting its address at Paulton in her journal: British Library Archive: Angela Carter Papers: Journal Add MS 88899/1/90:1965-1966.

221 Chris Torrance, 'An Interview with Glyn Pursglove.' *Poetry Wales* 19, no. 2 (1983): 134.

Torrance had a background in jazz, CND and beat poetry going back to the 1950s. In an interview conducted in 1977 he spoke of his desire to draw together all the poetry relating to his years in Bristol in a single volume but, to date, this has not happened.[222] He penned several portraits of the city, including a composition called 'Brandon Hill' with its imagist opening:

> Friday, sat on Brandon Hill & drank claret.
> It's hot, women push prams, boys play football.
> Old men patrol the park listlessly[223]

His eight-book poetic work *The Magic Door* (published 1973-1996, although some portions were written earlier during the Bristol years) is something of an unsung classic.

A lively programme of performance poetry complemented the vogue for small press printing in Bristol. Ian Breakwell (1943-2005) was perhaps most representative of this scene. He was a ground-breaking and influential poet and artist who wrote and staged radical experimental works during his time in Bristol. Breakwell put on regular performances at the Bristol Arts Centre in King Street during the 1960s. He contributed avant-garde multimedia productions, becoming one of the more renowned writers to emerge from the city's literary sub-culture. Yet more acclaimed was Barry Flanagan (1941-2009) who was later to collaborate with Breakwell and who also spanned the visual and performing arts. As a sculptor, poet and performer Flanagan contributed much to the cultural life of Clifton and its crescents during his relatively brief stay in the area. Of Welsh-Irish heritage, he moved to Bristol in 1959 and lived in the city until 1963 while he developed his sculptural practice and wrote concrete poetry. He supported his work by posing as a life model at the Bristol School of Art[224] at a time when other visual artists such as Richard Long and Peter Swan were starting their careers in the city. John James' warm tribute to Flanagan also evokes a powerful sense of his highly itinerant friend's bond with Bristol and provides a superb cameo of life in early 1960s Clifton and Hotwells:

> In 1962 and 1963 Barry Flanagan was a face on the streets of Bristol. A dandy *flâneur*, he would saunter out from his apartment on Cornwallis Crescent and stroll for miles of an evening, especially

222 Chris Torrance interviewed by Peter Hodgkiss (15 September 1977), published in *Poetry Information* 18 (1977-78).

223 Chris Torrance, *Green Orange Purple Red* (London: Ferry Press, 1968), 34.

224 Details from Barry Flanagan: Official website: http://barryflanagan.com/home/ [accessed 15 July 2018].

on the pavements of Clifton between the pale cream stone of serene buildings such as Royal York Crescent and West Mall. At night, below Clifton to the south, the lights of Hotwells next to the River Avon would illuminate the sky. Flanagan referred to Bristol as handsome, and the docks as reassuring. He had a special bond with the place, which he retained long after moving away. Jessica Sturgess, his partner of many years, told me that whenever they passed within its vicinity later, he would doff his hat to what he called the mother and father of all cities.[…] He would frequent the bohemian haunts of Bristol, such as the Blackboy Café on Blackboy Hill and the cider houses: the Quinton House in Clifton, the Cotham Porter Stores and the Ostrich in Hotwells. These were used by a heterogeneous community of prostitutes, Second World War veterans, working men, gangsters, students, artists and poets. He floated through this crowded *demimonde*.[225]

The Carters' friends Nick and Corinna Gray found that Barry and Sue Flanagan were among their neighbours in Cornwallis Crescent. The Grays and Flanagans got to know each other since Sue Flanagan (née Lewis) and Corinna both had home births facilitated by the same midwife who became a mutual acquaintance. Nick Gray recalled a hilarious incident when Flanagan exhibited at the Arnolfini art gallery:

My daughter's dog (with de-rigueur bow tie) pissed on one of Barry's sand- filled hemp cones. 'That's life for an artist', says Barry. 'You gotta live with the critics!' Later Barry visited us on our narrowboats at the Camden Lock and told us about the performance he planned sinking into the Thames playing a double bass.[226]

It seems that the sand-filled hemp cones that had failed to impress the Grays' discerning canine friend were among a number of works Flanagan exhibited in the mid-1960s inspired by the idea of 'pataphysics. Art critic Andrew Wilson attributes Flanagan's preoccupation with 'pataphysics to a discussion with poet Nick Wayte, who, as we have seen, was also a part of Clifton circles in the mid-1960s.[227] Shirley Cameron (later Angela

225 John James, 'The Poet of Life and Sculpture: Barry Flanagan I', *Tate etc.* 33.Autumn 2011 (1 September 2011): https://www.tate.org.uk/context-comment/articles/poet-life-and-sculpture [accessed 20 June 2011].
226 Nick Gray, e-mail to the author (5 June 2018).
227 Andrew Wilson, 'Barry Flanagan Ringn '66', Tate website (September 2011): http://www.tate.org.uk/art/artworks/flanagan-ringn-66-t13295 [accessed 20 June 2018].

Carter's friend in Bath), recalled that she and Flanagan would often be the only people left working late during the night at London's Saint Martin's art college and that he would 'wander around late at night talking about 'Pataphysics'.[228] 'Pataphysics (prefixed with a single quotation mark) can be defined as a science of the undefinable, derived from the writings of Alfred Jarry (1873-1907), a precursor of Dada and surrealism, and eventually gaining new life from the attentions of the Situationists. It is something of a joke for the cognoscenti that has lasted more than a century. 'Pataphysics was in the air of experimentation and discovery during the late 1960s, even appearing in The Beatles song 'Maxwell's Silver Hammer' after the idea captured Paul McCartney's interest.

Angela Carter added Alfred Jarry's play *Ubu Roi* to her reading for 1963,[229] and her interest in his work continued, for instance enjoying his idea that 'laughter is born out of the discovery of the contradictory' among extensive notes copied in July 1965.[230] Carter name-checked Jarry's key text *Exploits and Opinions of Doctor Faustrall Pataphysician* in one of the opening quotations for her surrealist novel *The Infernal Desire Machines of Doctor Hoffman* (first planned in 1969, although not published until 1972).[231]

I would speculate that this fascination with 'pataphysics, within what, as Dave Lawton noted, was the very small community of Clifton at that time, had a possible correlation with the unique expression of Mojoism, a spurious historical religion that gained a short-lived cult-following. Lawton described some of the antics of an alternative performance club set up by his circle of friends—including the artist Bob Gale and the actor Marcel Steiner and of which Angela was on the periphery—in a room above the Lansdown pub at 8 Clifton Road, Clifton. This group, remembered as the 'Not Club' by Lawton, but the 'Grot Club' by Bob Gale, was a very different gathering from the Carters' folk nights at the same venue.

> We also created a thing called the 'Not Club', a sort of anarchist situationist set up. So, we got up to all sorts of things. Marcel Steiner, who was an actor, we put him in a straightjacket and we lowered him on a piece of rope from the window of the upstairs room.[232]

228 Shirley Cameron, telephone interview with the author (8 November 2018).
229British Library Archive: Angela Carter Papers: Journal Add MS 88899/1/88:1962-1963?
230 Journal entry written on 14 July 1965, British Library Archive: Angela Carter Papers: Journal Add MS 88899/1/90:1965-1966.
231 Gordon, *Invention of Angela Carter*, 143. Jarry also appears in Carter's later novel *Nights at the Circus* (1984).
232 Dave Lawton, telephone interview with the author (18 January 2018).

Such a happening in the Lansdown, today a pleasant but unexceptional Clifton pub, may sound improbable considering the colossal foolhardiness and exhibitionism that would be needed. When the character of Marcel Steiner (1932-1999) is considered, however, it is absolutely possible. Steiner was later famous for touring the 'smallest theatre in the world', constructed as a sidecar for a 1950s Panther motorbike, which could accommodate a single theatre-goer. Created in 1971, its repertoire included adaptations of *Hamlet, King Kong, Jaws, War and Peace* and *A Tale of Two Cities*.[233] Steiner was also notorious for setting himself on fire, driving four-inch nails up his nose and getting naked at any opportunity. Mark Borkowski's story that he once scaled 'four floors up the front of an Edinburgh town-house'[234] to get to a party also helps to corroborate that the 18-stone Steiner was the man for such an exploit, and no doubt the initiator of the proceedings at the Lansdown, not the dupe.

The critical mass of such off-beat talent in Clifton drove forward a proliferation of new cultural forms and styles. Bob Gale had been involved in the folk scene and Centre 42, but by the mid-1960s felt that 'It was not going anywhere, so I was out of the folk scene and no longer wanted to be involved with it. By that time, I was more interested in jazz and rock'n'roll'. Looking for new challenges, he co-founded the 'Grot Club' in around 1965 to write sketches which were performed at the Lansdown. He and Marcel Steiner were the main writers, producing a new script every five to six weeks. Membership was fluid but also included Bob's brother Richard Gale, Mike Harvey (a Bristol artist), Candy (second name unknown), Dave Ricketts, Marcel Steiner, Dave Snow and another woman whose name could not be recalled. They would put on special alternative pantomimes at Christmas such as 'Robin Hood on Ice'. Angela Carter would come to the events that they put on.[235] Such events indicate that the local counterculture was where the boundaries between creative arts such as visual art, theatre, music and literature were being demolished and the components being reconstructed in the cause of radical experimentation.

The phenomenon of Mojoism was closely connected to the circle that put on the Grot Club performances. Just as 'pataphysics combined metaphysics and humour in a kind of crypto-philosophy, Mojoism seems to have used a similar combination to create a crypto-religion. The Danish Situationist Asger

233 Fabulously, it was last heard of travelling around India with Mandy Medlicott as recently as 2015 (16 years after its designer's death). See Devanathan Veerappan, 'UK theatre group brings King Kong to Madurai', *The Times of India* (22 February 2015).
234 Mark Borkowski, 'Giant Among Dwarves', *The Guardian* (2 August 1999).
235 All recollections and quotation in this paragraph from Bob Gale, telephone interview with the author (26 November 2018).

Jorn had even spoken of 'pataphysics as 'a religion in the making' during the early 1960s. Dave Lawton recounted:

> We created this thing called The Mojoism. Angela was in it. We used to sit in the Lansdown pub. But we had to knock it on the head. And Dave Snow had made this little thing that you'd hang around your neck, like a little pendulum thing, made out of wood, you see. And people would ask 'What's that then?' And Dave'd say, 'Oh, it's a Mojo'. And we had all this Mojo poetry. And it was like swinging the great Mojo around. We used to say that the Mojo was discovered near Bath, near Radstock, years and years ago, hundreds of years ago by this guy called John of Bersack, and he was a Mojoist and they only drank wine and they'd get Mojoed. And that someone found this box with all this information; it's all a made-up story. Bill Fraser created this book, a 'Book of Mojo', we were all into this sort of stuff. And Bob decided to have a meeting for all these unassuming people who wanted to join the Mojoism. And we had these reflective shields. Angela was there, doing all this Mojo poetry, poetry that was supposed to be so powerful that you had to have deflective shields. It totally freaked us out. Because we realised that making a thing like that up, how people were taken in by it. But we used to do performances you know and things like that. We'd created situations and that was a kind of situation. But it got a bit out of hand, so we didn't go along with that.[236]

Any such improvisations that Angela Carter may have created now seem to have been lost. Bob Gale also remembers this 'manifestation' of Mojoism in the Clifton area during the mid-1960s but concedes 'there were three or four of us going around although I never quite figured out what it was about!'[237]

Bristol was to gain a reputation as a centre for experimental drama during the 1960s and 1970s. The emerging playwrights with close connections to the Clifton area during the period were to achieve national renown. Tom Stoppard lived in Bristol during the 1950s and 1960s, mostly developing his craft as a writer while working as a local reporter. It might be expected that the two writers, Carter and Stoppard, would have met, since Stoppard mixed widely in the same neighbourhood. Ian A. Anderson, for example, encountered Tom Stoppard in Royal York Crescent:

236 Dave Lawton, telephone interview with the author (18 January 2018).
237 Bob Gale, telephone interview with the author (26 November 2018).

I remember a theatrically-connected family who lived along there, the elder daughter of which was briefly my girlfriend. [...] I remember being invited for supper one night and finding that another visitor was a young up and coming playwright called Tom Stoppard.[238]

Carter and Stoppard did not share the same circle but seemed to revolve around each other in 1960s Clifton. Gordon cites a reference from Carter mentioning that she saw Stoppard once 'across a crowded room'.[239] Moreover, Neil Curry remarks that 'Tom Stoppard rarely seemed to speak' and 'was in silent evidence (Angela mistook his silence for being boring) at various parties'.[240] Carter's limited encounters with Bristolian playwright Peter Nichols seems to hinge upon more direct cross-communication since she later clashed with him over responses to her friend Salman Rushdie's *Satanic Verses*, of which she was a great admirer and stout defender. Most famous for *A Day in the Death of Joe Egg* (1967), Nichols's *The Gorge* (1968) was also filmed in the city, and brilliantly captures the highs and lows of a family day out from Bristol to the Cheddar Gorge. Other notable Bristol-based playwrights active from the 1960s onwards, with renown that reached beyond the city, include A. C. H. Smith and Charles Wood (perhaps most famous for The Beatles film *Help!*). As we have seen, St George-born scriptwriter Bob Baker (whose productions include episodes of *Dr Who*, the Bristol-based detective series *Shoestring* and Ardman Animations classics) also lived in Clifton throughout the period.

Theatre of an even more alternative nature was popular in Bristol during the 1960s and 1970s. Both of the earliest English underground theatre companies, CAST (Cartoon Archetypical Slogan Theatre) and the People Show, were known for their experimental and political approach and had connections to the city. Claire Muldoon (née Burnley) and Roland Muldoon founded the influential socialist collective known as CAST in 1965, after they met during their involvement with the Bristol Old Vic Theatre School.[241] The People Show, founded in 1966 by Jeff Nuttall, prominent in the English underground as the author of *Bomb Culture*, regularly performed at Bristol Arts Centre and the Albany Theatre from 1967 onwards. The company was

238 Ian A. Anderson, e-mail to the author (2 July 2018).
239 From the *New Review* (July 1977), cited in Gordon, *Invention of Angela Carter*, 53.
240 Neil Curry, e-mails to the author (3 and 5 October 2018).
241 Andy Curtis, *Unfinished Histories: Recording the History of Alternative Theatre* website, 'CAST': https://www.unfinishedhistories.com/history/companies/cast/ [accessed 31 January 2019]. Roland Muldoon became politicised while living in Clifton and working as a building worker and electrician's mate, during which time he encountered several Marxists and became involved with the New Left.

closely connected to the Arts Lab movement and was soon joined by Roland Miller, Angela Carter's friend and collaborator in performance art during the 1970s.

Two unorthodox theatre groups, the Crystal Theatre of the Saint and Sistershow, particularly exemplified home-grown alternative theatre. That such initiatives were being generated and thriving within Bristol indicates a dynamic counterculture with suitable locations, effective promotion and a substantial network of support to sustain them over several years.

The Crystal Theatre of the Saint was innovative, influential and ran for a decade, staging events in Bristol and on tour across Europe. Paul Basset Davies and Bradley Winterton set up the company in 1971, first performing a play called *Gibbous Moon* at the University of Bristol's Anson Room in Queen's Road, Clifton in 1971. Bristol's underground paper *Seeds* provided an enthusiastic early review, admiring the authentic and experimental approach:

> For once we really have got a 'happening' which isn't just a second-rate imitation of something else but something new and exciting.[242]

The venture developed into an independent cooperative and created what must have been an intriguing ambience. Their multimedia performances combined original scripts with elements of surrealism and Grateful Dead style light shows illuminating activities on stage, while the company's members played live music. For three years from 1976, the Crystal Theatre of the Saint squatted a warehouse near Temple Meads which they named the 'Otherperson Hotel', continuing their live performances and putting on large parties, anticipating the acid house raves a decade later. In 1979 they returned to Clifton, to reside at Worcester Terrace, where they formed the rock band, Shoes for Industry.[243] While the Crystal Theatre of the Saint had ended by 1981, it can claim an impact nationally and internationally as well as within Bristol. Its legacy consisted of inspiration for existing and new productions, while former company members also took their creative abilities into new projects and spheres.

In 1973 another alternative theatre troupe, Sistershow, sprang up singing, dancing and shouting from the counterculture. Jackie Thrupp, Pat VT West

242 [Anon.], 'Crystal Theatre of the Saint', *Seeds* 3 [1971], 12. Additional details from *Unfinished Histories: Recording the History of Alternative Theatre* website, 'Crystal Theatre of the Saint': http://www.unfinishedhistories.com/history/companies/crystal-theatre-of-the-saint/ [accessed 17 July 2018].
243 See also Loats and Sprinks, *Bristol Boys Make More Noise!*, 144-151. Shoes for Industry attracted the attention of John Peel, once recording a set for one of his renowned sessions.

and other members of the Bristol Women's Liberation Group launched Sistershow at the Bower Ashton Campus of the then Bristol Polytechnic in March 1973. The event was a fund-raiser for the Bristol Women's Centre, where the group came to be based at 11 Waverley Road, Redland. In the DIY spirit, Sistershow members wrote their own material and designed the sets for performances enlivened by lashings of feminist agit-prop. The formula of a revue format presented as multimedia happenings, accompanied by Monica Sjöö's and Beverly Skinner's artwork, proved to be hugely popular. The full story of this feminist extravaganza with attitude is told in *Sistershow Revisited*, a collection of writings on the group edited by Deborah Withers to accompany the *Sistershow Revisited* exhibition and programme of events held at the Centrespace Gallery in 2011. Sistershow's blaze of glory was short-lived, ending in 1975, but the creative energy continued through numerous other projects and was fondly remembered by those involved.

Dissident Voices:
Bristolians Unite! You have only your chainstores to lose...

A world safe for anarchists to live in.[244]

Bristol began to achieve a reputation for radicalism and activism during the decade that Angela Carter lived in the city. The celebrated Bristol Bus Boycott of 1963 was a significant campaign and victory against racial discrimination. Its successful outcome was a milestone in the struggle for civil rights in England. 1968 saw the first St Pauls Carnival, while Bristol University students and other anti-racist campaigners gave Enoch Powell a hostile reception when he spoke in Chippenham on 11th May, shortly after his notorious 'Rivers of blood' speech.[245] When the Springboks rugby team, representing racially segregated South Africa, came to play at the Horfield Memorial ground in 1969, Bristol Anti-Apartheid activists staged a mass protest and even delayed the match by sprinkling tacks on the pitch.[246] As we have seen, there were also

244 British Library Archive: Angela Carter Papers: Journal Add MS 88899/1/88:1962-1963?, entry for July 8th.
245 'Bristol Students Mob Powell', *Bristol Evening Post* (25 May 1968).
246 See James Belsey, '550 Police for the Springboks', *Bristol Evening Post* (5 December 1969), 1; 'Springboks—Plan to Invade Ground', *Bristol Evening Post* (5 December 1969), 2; Colin Thomas, 'Bringing the Fight Against Apartheid to Bristol', *Bristol Cable* 12 (12 August 2017): https://thebristolcable.org/2017/08/bringing-fight-apartheid-bristol/ [accessed 30 December 2018]; Ron Press, *Ron Press: His Story –To Change the World! Is Reason Enough?* [unpublished autobiography, London: 1995]: https://thebristolcable.org/wp-content/uploads/2017/08/12-To-Change-the-World-is-Reason-Enough.doc.pdf [accessed 30 December 2018], [35].

prominent marches and concerts against nuclear weapons and the Vietnam War in Bristol. 1968 was a particularly significant year. There were local demonstrations for solidarity with the May 1968 uprising in Paris. Industrial relations were turbulent, with a confident and organised labour movement undertaking effective strike action, including a major dispute at Rolls Royce. The Bristol Radical History Festival, held at the city's M Shed in May 2018, marked the anniversary of the tumultuous political events that occurred across the world fifty years earlier. The event included speakers who shared their experiences of participation in the other headline activism of that year: the major student occupation at the University of Bristol in December 1968. After the last whiff of tear-gas had dispersed in Paris following May 1968, the mood of change and spirit of resistance reappeared across the world, expressed through demonstrations, sit-ins, factory-gate assemblies and free festivals. Bristol was no exception.

It is valuable to consider the late 1960s and early 1970s in their own terms, however inevitable it is that present-day debates may influence our understanding. To embed the discussion in the preoccupations of that period it is helpful, therefore, to take notice of some of the tensions that were evident at the time. A debate in an article produced for the University of Bristol's *Nonesuch News* in 1971 gives a platform to three perspectives held within the campus politics of the day.[247] It is an informative and illuminating exchange which shows both divisions in student politics and wider tensions within the counterculture. Representing the establishment, Michael Wigmore, Vice-Chairman of the Conservative Association, praises Enoch Powell's 'exciting personality' and claims to uphold the values of 'Free Enterprise, personal liberty and free speech'. Wigmore suggests that 'hippies have less in common with the Revolutionaries than a lamb with a tarantula'. The second commentator, one 'P. Toker', claims to represent the counterculture. 'P. Toker' rejects 'anarchical violence', the use of LSD and 'attitude change' as short-cuts to overthrow the present system. For 'P. Toker':

> Waiting is the only answer for us—waiting for the split in the walls of society, the beginnings of its self-destruction, becoming as fully aware and capable as possible to cope with the ultimate and predictable revolution and the consequent re-establishing of a society which we could participate in.

[247]All references to this article from 'The Counter Culture & Socialism. Two Ideologies? The Lamb and the Tarantula', *Nonesuch News* (22 October 1971), 6 in University of Bristol Special Collections Archive: DM 976 Nonesuch News 1966-1970 with gaps 1970-1972.

'P. Toker' also attacks environmental destruction and alienation, suggesting the futility of party politics as an effective pathway to change.

By contrast, the third commentator, an anonymous revolutionary socialist, explored the tensions between the counterculture and the programme of the new left, being 'very critical' of aspects of the countercultural approach. Although conceding that 'there are some progressive elements that could emerge from it', this commentator charges that:

> The dominant ideas of the counter-culture are those of the radical middle class: un-critical liberalism, anti-intellectualism and a rather bogus anti-materialism.

The revolutionary socialist is not wholly dismissive of the counterculture, however, noting that prominent underground papers such as *OZ*, *IT* and *Ink* had become increasingly politicised, with signs that attacks upon them were provoking a fight back. Furthermore, this commentator is supportive of the way that underground papers have engaged with 'radical community politics and giving support to various left groups like Women's Lib, Gay Lib and so on'.

The article's editor supports a synthesis of the 'dropouts' of the counterculture and revolutionary socialist ideas on the grounds that there was a 'very real political threat posed by the anti-materialist ethos and lifestyle of the "counterculture", and the need for Socialists to consider the issues of ends and means raised by the underground movement'. The editor concludes by expressing the hope that the 'tarantula' of revolutionary socialism and the 'lamb' of the counterculture (an awkward metaphor!) will fight together. In the next decade a resurgent Conservative government was to attack both the militant organised labour movement, most prominently in the miners' strike, partly fought out in nearby south Wales, and east London's Wapping

---

Facing page:
Top left—Striking Filton aircraft workers demanded immediate substantial pay increases, 3 weeks annual holiday and equal pay for women. Ernest Brown, Harry Wright, Secretary, and Viv Ryan on Brandon Hill, 15 March 1968 (*Evening Post*).
Top right—Protesting against the Engineering Employers' Federation blockage of a wage claim during the Filton aircraft engineers' strike. Captioned 'Woman in a man's world', 15 March 1968 (*Evening Post*).
Bottom—Assembly of striking engineers on Bristol's Brandon Hill, 15 March 1968 (*Evening Post*).

dispute and the most unruly wing of the counterculture, in the form of the free festival travellers known as The Convoy, during the so-called Battle of the Beanfield, near Amesbury. Elements of both revolutionary socialism and the counterculture were present in the successful fight back against the poll tax five years later.

Throughout her adult life Angela Carter was a stalwart opponent of conservatism. Neil Curry's perception was that initially 'Paul was the political one, Angela's politics were more emotional than thought through'.[248] This may have been true of her older husband's influence during the early to mid-1960s, but Angela was to develop into an engaged and articulate critic on political and cultural matters. Her socialist politics were at once sincere and steadfast, yet also flexible and exploratory.

Angela Carter put herself through a vigorous political self-education programme during her decade in Bristol. Her journals from the 1960s itemise her reading matter, which included works by or about Herbert Marcuse, Hegel, Roland Barthes, Alex Comfort, Theodore Adorno, Walter Benjamin, Tzvetan Todorov and an intensive reading of the works of Marx and Engels. Her politics were also influenced by her experiences in Bristol and discussions with people around her who were coming to terms with a society in transition. Social and economic conflicts were played out in tensions between tendencies that were idealistic, traditionalist, commercial and outright anti-social at the neighbourhood level. Carter's fictional counterculture featured the ruthless Honeybuzzard, the unanchored but mostly well-meaning Joseph Harker and the vulnerable Annabel Collins. The society of contemporary 1960s Clifton that they reflected was definitely not utopian. Yet a freewheeling spirit seeking possibilities for radical social reorganisation and creativity could also shine through. Bob Gale described a project he was involved with as follows:

> There was a certain element of altruism in the sixties (a lot of people that were totally cut-throat as well, perhaps even worse than today). Myself and two friends opened an art gallery in Clifton, in York Place. We had the top of a garage in a really good location. We would put on people's work and not charge. We did have an exhibition. We even paid for the gallery. I don't even know how we managed this at the time, because we really had no money. It was very humdrum, but it really worked.[249]

248 Neil Curry, e-mail to the author (5 October 2018).
249 Bob Gale, telephone interview with the author (26 November 2018).

Gordon Strong also reflected on his mixed experience of the alternative society he encountered when he moved to Bristol, its entrancing idealism, its important political edge, but also the increasingly detrimental impact of commercialism and elements of elitism that had impacted on the underground circles in London from the later 1960s. I quote in length from my interview in which Strong described the shifting nature of the counterculture that he found, since it at once celebrates the empowering influence of the West Country's 'provincial bohemia' but also identifies some of the conflicts and contradictions which I have been exploring:

> I was born in a tiny little village, in Brean, which was a tiny community and going to Bristol was like going to Mars or something. It was a huge thing for me, and a very good one. Because you met people from all over England, and from other countries, so it was a big revelation, a huge revelation.
>
> Bristol is a very conservative city, with the Merchant Venturers and all that stuff. I mean if the counterculture was going to happen at all, it would happen in Clifton because that was the closest thing to an alternative society.
>
> I think the thing is to try to put things in context. I mean why [the counterculture] was so different, although it didn't appear to be different. It just developed organically. When it works, it works, but these things are always psychic. And people always forget the bad bits.
>
> I mean it's interesting because the '60s, the late '60s, it was still just about there in 1970, and then it started to go downhill. After the early Pilton [festival] was the swan song, because money started to get involved, how are people going to live? Who's going to make money out of this? And the idealism just faded away.[250]

As we have seen, Angela Carter was strongly connected to the left-wing political activism that Strong encountered, as well as creative arts. There have long been rumours that Carter spent time within Bristol anarchist circles during her time as a student at the University of Bristol. Christopher Frayling recalled that:

250 Gordon Strong, interview with the author (La Ruca Café, Gloucester Road, Bristol 28 February 2019).

The Berkeley café in Bristol's Queens Road.

She once reminisced that her political formation grew partly from her childhood experiences in South Yorkshire and its coalfields during the War, and partly from conversations with her anarchist friends in Bristol who would meet at the Berkeley Café opposite the university.[251]

Neil Curry's published poem 'To Ms Angela Carter, The Berkeley Café, Bristol', confirms that the café was his friend's regular place to chat, observe life and joke with the waiters.[252] Dave Lawton, an anarchist friend of Angela and Paul Carter during the 1960s also spent time in The Berkeley in Queens Road. Now a Wetherspoons pub, The Berkeley had a varied past from being a shopping arcade to an upmarket entertainment venue with a ballroom and tea-room. Lawton shared some reminiscences of the habitués of the late 1960s:

251 Frayling, *Inside the Bloody Chamber*, 37. In Frayling's more recent published account, the reference has been edited to the unspecific 'in a café opposite the Wills Building', see 'Christopher Frayling, 'A Bath Literary Friendship' pp. 12-17 in *Strange Worlds: The Vision of Angela Carter*, ed. by Marie Mulvey Roberts and Fiona Robinson (Bristol: Samson & Co./ Redcliffe, 2016), 17.
252 Neil Curry, *Some Letters Never Sent'* (London: Enitharmon Press, 2014), pp. 25-26. See also Gordon, *The Invention of Angela Carter*, 72-73.

Oh, The Berkeley, yes! There was a guy called [X] who used to be there. He'd had a breakdown. He was an amazing guy, totally off his trolley. And he used to go in The Berkeley. And he'd been an accountant in Africa. I remember one time, he would make himself a suit out of newspapers, and he'd walk around Park Street. But, anyway, he used to come in The Berkeley, and we'd all be sitting round the table having a cup of tea and that. And [X] would go 'So & so & so & so on the 3 o'clock'. And everyone would rush to the bookies to put money on it. Because every time he was right. He was like totally off his trolley, but psychic. And he knew what horse was going to win.

And so, yes, we'd go in The Berkeley. And it became quite notorious too in the late 60s and the 70s in the acid scene. We used to get this guy called [X] who was, really, picking up young girls and farming them out to strip clubs and stuff. So we got on to him. He was a headbanger and what did we do? Yes, we stopped his acid supply and we pulled his trousers down.[253]

Susannah Clapp put even more stress on the significance of the anarchists and situationists at The Berkeley than Frayling. She recorded that:

And in the Berkeley Café [...] she chatted to situationists and anarchists. As we sat in her kitchen in April 1991, ten months before she died, Angela said these anarchists had had more influence than anyone else on her politics.[254]

So how did Angela Carter's encounters with anarchists come about? Anarchist Stuart Christie records that the Bristol Anarchist Group, particularly Mike 'Digger' Walsh and Ian Vine (?-2010) hosted a national gathering on

---

253 Dave Lawton, telephone interview with the author (18 January 2018). In the later 1970s and 1980s, there were regular concerts upstairs in the Berkeley Café, including, Richard Jones believes, seminal gigs as the Bristol sound developed with listings that included the likes of The Pop Group and The Cortinas. Richard Jones, personal conversation with the author 21 July 2018 (Bristol Harbour Festival). A gig list belonging to Richard Wyatt and published online, records that Echo and The Bunnymen, Nine Below Zero and even U2 played at The Berkeley, Bristol Archive Records, 'Gigs 1978-1985': http://www.bristolarchiverecords.com/gigs2.html [accessed 2 October 2018]. See also Loats and John Sprinks, *Bristol Boys Make More Noise!*, 196.
254 Clapp, *A Card from Angela Carter*, 51.

anarchism under the auspices of the Anarchist Federation of Britain in 1964.[255] This gathering took place at the new Arnolfini Gallery, which as we have seen, was initially set up on The Triangle in Clifton. Bristol, alongside London and Manchester, was one of the most significant hotspots for English anarchist activity. Dave Thorne, a long-term friend of Angela Carter, became involved with the group at this time:

> It was then that I became involved with quite a number of the anarchists who stayed on in Bristol, and Bristol actually became an important place for anarchists, including people like Stuart Christie, the anarchist who went to Spain, he stayed in Bristol for some time.[256]

As we have seen, Dave Thorne and Pat Thorne had bought the house at 49 Cotham Brow together with John Orsborn and Jenny Orsborn in 1963. John Orsborn introduced them to Angela Carter when they attended an auction in Bristol together. They remained good friends with Carter after she left the West Country for Clapham, and until the end of her life. The Thornes were a direct link, therefore, to the Bristol anarchist circles since they knew Ian Vine and introduced Carter to 'Digger' Walsh and another prominent Bristol anarchist, Adam Nicholson, who eventually started what was probably Bristol's first wholefood and macrobiotic food stall (which also distributed anarchist literature) at St Nicholas Market. The Thornes believe that Carter is likely to have continued further discussions with anarchists at the University of Bristol, where she was a student until 1965, as much as at The Berkeley. The only character cited as an anarchist in the Bristol trilogy is Bruno, a minor figure who the unreliable Honeybuzzard designates as such and as 'partly Lithuanian', and who features among a gang of stoned and drunk beatniks in *Shadow Dance*.[257] Carter always disguised the identities of any characters who were adapted from real-life Bristolians. Pat Thorne believes that Bruno was in fact based upon a local Polish man called Fred Siemaszko because he

255 Stuart Christie, *My Granny Made Me an Anarchist: The Christie File Vol. 1, 1946-1964*, 2nd rev. ed. (Hastings: Christie Books, 2002), 179. Vine is listed as the contact for the Bristol Federation at an address in Hotwells in *Freedom* 24 22(13 July 1963): https://freedomnews. org.uk/wp-content/uploads/2018/03/Freedom-1963-07-13.pdf [accessed 8 February 2019]. As we have seen, his investigative journalism was to challenge the police action at The Three Tuns. Vine also wrote a collection of poetry entitled *Cascades,* published in Hotwells, Bristol in 1965.

256 Pat Thorne and Dave Thorne, Skype interview with the author (28 January 2019). Stuart Christie had become notorious as an eighteen-year old when he attempted to assassinate the Spanish dictator Francisco Franco.

257 Carter, *Shadow Dance*, 111.

'was connected to John Osborn. They would have been part of that little clique together', while Dave Thorne added 'he was more English than that the rest of us, so we called him "English Fred"'. Pat and Dave Thorne have, therefore, been able to provide first-hand corroboration of Carter's social connections to the Bristol anarchist circles during the 1960s.

With strong socialist leanings, Angela Carter once described herself as 'in a slap-dash kind of way an anarcho-Marxist',[258] a political orientation that seems to have developed during her coffee house and pub discussions in and around the University of Bristol. The spectacle of unshackled revolutionary *joie de vivre* fascinated and heartened her although she described it from the point of view of a bystander. In the following account of a street rally in London, probably in 1963, for example, Carter does not join the dancing throng but remains an, perhaps envious, observer:

> The splinter-group of anarchists danced rather than marched past up at Hyde Park, the girls' plaits bouncing, & all their muddy boots ruthless on the poor old tortured grass & their dark spectacles glassily reflecting the sunless day & some of them were blowing away at penny whistles like Indian music &, all told, one could tell something was up.

> West Indians twisting along to a steel band; young girls tumbled off the pavement to dance with them. Joy, it really was.[259]

While she was open to, and broadly in sympathy with, left-wing socialist and anarchist ideas, she was not a banner-carrying activist in the manner of contemporaries in Clifton, such as Monica Sjöö or founder Greenham Common woman Ann Pettitt. Carter was uncomfortable with fixed political labels which are near absent from her early novels. Carter's self-identification with anarchism—elsewhere she referred to 'various intellectual adventures in anarcho-surrealism'[260]—and revolutionary causes seems to have had a slightly throwaway, off-hand quality, as if to wrongfoot potential opponents by provocation, rather than being an expression of a thoroughgoing political conviction. In *Love*, Lee and Buzz Collins are inspired by their aunt's Marxism to support the Cuban revolution when teenagers, yet socialism features little in

258 Letter to Marion Boyars received 9 October 1972, quoted in Anna Watz, *Angela Carter and Surrealism: 'A Feminist Libertarian Aesthetic'* (London: Routledge, 2017), 1.
259 British Library Archive: Angela Carter Papers: Journal Add MS 88899/1/88:1962-1963?, entry for April 21st.
260 Carter, 'Notes From the Front Line' in *Shaking a Leg*, 37.

their adult lives. In a letter written in 1972, moreover, she stated that she was sceptical about revolutionary projects: 'My position in *any* [Carter's emphasis] revolution, sexual or otherwise, is always bound to be equivocal because I, basically, don't want to get involved'.[261] This equivocation, stems perhaps from a disaffection that made her reluctant to substitute one set of rules and rulers with another supposedly more revolutionary alternative.

While Angela Carter retained an ironic, writerly distance her sympathies were secure and political acumen impressive. Pat Thorne recalled:

> she was immensely well-informed. Whenever you had a political discussion with her, she was absolutely informed on her subject. I mean long before I had heard about East Timor, she knew all about it.[262]

It is fitting that the memorial event held at the Ritzy Cinema in Brixton as a tribute to Angela Carter's life, following her funeral in 1992, was a cultural and political event. Dave Thorne and Pat Thorne recalled the unexpected appearance of Salman Rushdie in the aftermath of the *Satanic Verses* controversy:

> Tariq Ali was there. Salman Rushdie turned up late, and nobody knew he was going to be there, because it was at the time of the fatwa. He came with a police escort. He slipped in and spoke. So, they played the eight records [that Angela had chosen for Radio 4's *Desert Island Discs*], and people spoke in between, including Salman Rushdie.[263]

To take a step back to the 1960s, Carter studied at the University of Bristol, mostly based in Clifton from 1962 to 1965, so was no longer based there when the great student occupation sparked off in 1968. I have found no evidence that she either participated or commented upon what was to be the most prominent political mobilisation in Clifton during the late 1960s.

---

261 Letter to Carole Roffe, 11 January 1972, quoted in Gordon, *Invention of Angela Carter*, 164.
262 Pat Thorne and Dave Thorne, Skype interview with the author (28 January 2019).
263 Pat Thorne and Dave Thorne, Skype interview with the author (28 January 2019).

Erupting Beautifully: The 1968 Student Occupation

At Hornsey and Bristol years of isolated complaint and grumbling erupted beautifully.[264]

More than 800 students occupied the University's Senate House in a sustained sit-in from 5th-16th December 1968. While student activism in Bristol may have followed in the wake of that elsewhere, the University buildings located in the Clifton area became the site of one of the major standoffs in the late 1960s era of student resistance. The main demands were altruistic and radical. The broader attack was upon the 'binary' mentality that imposed a two-tiered hierarchical system in higher education. Immediate objectives included not only making the University's decision-making structures more democratic and expanding the existing student union provision but extending access to all of Bristol's students. The inclusive demand for 'reciprocal arrangements' sought to open up facilities to those at Bristol Polytechnic and local technical colleges. The first skirmishes in the battle with the University authorities, represented by the Senate Committee, took place in a brief occupation in June 1968. This debacle was linked to the creation of a 'free university' project, modelled on those previously set up in Cambridge and London. The *International Times* reported that the New-Left inspired initiative quickly developed into a 'large and non-sectarian grouping' of around 500 people organising a regular programme of events on campus.[265] The series of lectures and discussions led to an early clash in the first week when the University attempted to close down the student union buildings to its students at the weekend. After some further discussion, the students involved responded by refusing to leave the building. This brief sit-in was a prelude to the more extensive occupation of December 1968.

For all its casualties, egotism and the eventual recuperation of key parts of the counterculture, the confidence manifest in such moments of collective action to seize and change the prevailing circumstances are inspiring. The 1968 occupations were audacious attempts to experience an alternative existence in the here and now and to wrest a different future reality. University of Bristol students who supported the sit-in (not all of them) did so to complain about the 'gross unfairness in the proportion of money available'[266] to themselves

---

264 David Widgery (ed.) *The Left in Britain 1956-68* (Harmondsworth: Penguin, 1976), 315.

265 Ian Vine, report in *International Times* (1.35 (July 1968). See *International Times Archive:* http://www.internationaltimes.it/archive/page.php?i=IT_1968-07-12_B-IT-Volume-1_Iss-35_002&view=text

266 [Staff reporters], 'Student Sit-in Ends and Then Another One Starts', *The Times* (6 December 1968), 2 [online] *Times Digital Archive.*

'Students holding banners hide their faces as they demonstrate in front of Senate House today', *Evening Post* (December 1968). Banner captions read 'Free people govern themselves', 'Our union, our education', 'solidarity support', 'End the binary system', 'What will you say when your children ask: what did you do to democratise higher education?' and in tribute to their comrades in Paris 'lutte [continue?]'.

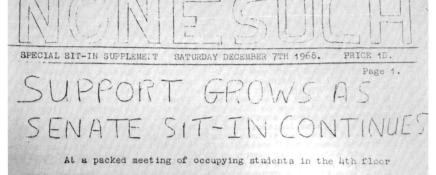

SPECIAL SIT-IN SUPPLEMENT   SATURDAY DECEMBER 7TH 1968.   PRICE 1D.

Page 1.

SUPPORT GROWS AS SENATE SIT-IN CONTINUES

At a packed meeting of occupying students in the 4th floor common room of Senate House at 10p.m. on Friday night, a motion calling for an end to the sit-in at 12 noon on Saturday (culminating in a demonstration march back to the Union)was overwhelmingly defeated, and thus the sit-in continues indefinitely. A large body of students opposed to the sit-in were present at this meeting and the numbers were swelled to over a thou sand.

The proposer of the motion, Mr Duce, said that the point of the sit-in had been made, the only further point in staying would be if doing so would be likely to force the Vice-Chancellor into granting reciprocal membership. This was not likely to happen.

Sit-in special of the University of Bristol paper *Nonesuch News*, produced during the Occupation (7 December 1968).

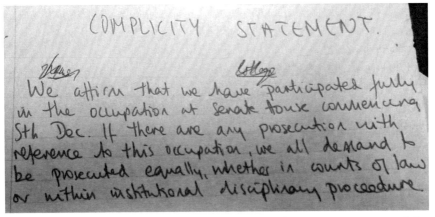

'We all demand to be prosecuted equally': complicity statement signed by Bristol University occupiers in 1968.

'It keeps them off the streets': cartoon from University of Bristol student paper *Nonesuch News*, published 28 February 1969 in the aftermath of the December 1968 sit-in.

in comparison to that enjoyed by other students in the area. For student radicals, occupation was not just a physical take-over of a building but a transformative state of mind that took them beyond the expected conventions of academic life. Rather than spectating from the side-lines, to be occupied is to be fully engaged and participating in the moment. They were at once taking a space but also exploring modes of mass participation. In this way they were striking a blow against individual competition and alienation. As the title of Carter's 1968 novel *Several Perceptions* suggests, more than one reality and multiple outcomes are possible. Hearing first-hand accounts from those who were involved in such events brings to life some of the spirit of the 'festal' atmosphere that she felt in Bristol at the time. Student occupiers Sue Tate and Kevin Whitson shared their reminiscences and reflections at the Bristol Radical History Festival at the City's M Shed fifty years later in May 2018, describing how the act of pooling and asserting imaginative demands brought into being the potential for further possibilities. Tate recalled, for example, that whatever the shortcomings of the occupation, one outcome was that 'hundreds of students had an experience of participatory democracy'. This is no small thing. Such an impact is not futile, despite the overwhelming weight of hindsight regarding the way that we might subsequently consider the failures in the realisation of students' demands.

Under the auspices of a steering group, the students set up a general assembly in Senate House to conduct debates and to organise the campaign. This was attended by University of Bristol's own students, a small number of staff and was also open to other students, in keeping with the principle to support 'reciprocal arrangements'. The sense of participation in events that were extraordinary and unique was no doubt enhanced by the fact that the first discussions were held by the light of hurricane lamps and candles, since an early response by the University establishment was to cut electricity to the building (the local fire brigade quickly intervened to insist that the electric lights were restored as a matter of public safety). Sue Tate recalled that, while the Steering Committee was male-dominated, several women also took prominent roles, including herself as press officer. This, she found, attracted considerable comment in the media. The main force of the students' challenge to Vice-Chancellor Prof. Roderick Collar and the University establishment was against the 'class-ridden' nature of higher education, rejecting the class division between the old university and the new polytechnics.

The memories that Tate retained from the heady days of early December 1968 were fond ones:

It was just so exciting. It really was fun. Senate House with Beatles playing, some people screen printing, some people running around and feeding each other and meeting people you'd never met before. And we believed we were making history. I don't remember much factionalism; it was really exploratory, people were trying to think it through… what was going on and how do we understand and where might we turn for more information and more understanding?[267]

In addition to the immediate concerns of the sit-in, broader questions about social power were in question. In the aftermath of the 'événements' in Paris, and across the world, the possibility of a thoroughgoing social revolution was on the agenda. Several far-reaching issues were at stake in the occupation at the University of Bristol and the students concerned were conscious that they were involved in actions that were a part of an international struggle that had reached its high-point on the streets of Paris six months earlier. Sue Tate confirmed that 'We were very aware of what had been going on in Paris and we felt part of that. At one point Cohn-Bendit was going to visit us and then he didn't and we were very disappointed'.[268] At the most revolutionary end of the spectrum Monica Sjöö put up a poster produced by King Mob (the English section of the Situationist International, which had helped to instigate the May 1968 uprising which had rocked the French Establishment) during a sit-in at Senate House on 1st December 1968 and got together with 'rebel students' including Ann Pettitt to create more King Mob influenced posters.[269] The occupation was over by mid-December. Afterwards the Senate Committee threatened legal repercussions for those activists that it regarded as ringleaders. When prominent student activists were threatened with legal action in the wake of the occupation, many of their peers signed a complicity statement in solidarity to help rebuff charges against individuals. Occupier Gordon Strong noted that 'Bizarrely, the University denied the existence of this complicity statement throughout and after the sit-in'.[270] Not all students, however, were deterred from efforts to bring about positive change and Tate records that camps and free schools continued over several years following the

267 Sue Tate and Kevin Whitson, 'The Bristol Sit-in: Student protest and occupation in 1968', talk at Bristol Radical History Festival, M Shed Bristol (6 May 2018): https://www.brh.org.uk/site/events/studio-2-you-say-you-want-a-revolution-student-protest-and-occupation-in-bristol-may-1968/ [accessed 2 December 2018].
268 Tate and Whitson, 'The Bristol Sit-in'.
269 White, Monica Sjöö: *Life and Letters*, 45.
270 Complicity statement from University of Bristol Special Collections: Student Occupations DM 1635/ Box 2 Sit-in 1968. Gordon Strong's comment from unpublished lecture 'Senate House Sit-In 1968'. [nd].

Bristol march in solidarity with French students, Victoria Rooms, 25 May 1968 (*Evening Post*).

sit-in, as former student occupiers 'reached out to kids from deprived areas in the city'.[271] For Kevin Whitson, reflecting on the 1968 events in retrospect, while class was an explicit focus of the occupation, the enduring legacy of the 1960s counterculture more generally was a great impact in cultural matters 'where it contributed towards a significant shift', despite its limited impact in a party political sense.[272] The emerging social movements integrated the politics of gender in a more thoroughgoing way than that of the older left and indeed of the New Left. The spirit of student activism also contributed towards the momentum for the opening-up of education during the immediately succeeding decades.

271 Tate and Whitson, 'The Bristol Sit-in'.
272 Tate and Whitson, 'The Bristol Sit-in'.

The Bristol Dwarfs

The Bristol Dwarfs, as we have seen, in part hailed from the home of John Orsborn, the prototype for Angela Carter's Honeybuzzard and her one-time lover. The appearance of the Dwarfs in early 1971, albeit as a tiny group and party, is significant because it indicates that Bristol was up with the times in terms of a pan-European phenomenon linking it to London and Amsterdam and that Clifton was connected in turn to the early flowering of the environmental direct-action movement. The Dwarfs were instrumental in the West Country gaining a reputation as the heart of the festival counterculture in the British Isles, being initiators of both the early Bristol Free Festival in Clifton and the Stonehenge People's Free Festival which, by the final gathering, had reached epic proportions when up to 30,000 festival-goers camped near the stone circle for a month in June 1984.

An account by 'Rustic' Rod Goodway of Magic Muscle captures the spirit of Bristol's Dwarf Party:

> We also got involved with street politics and started out doing work for the Black Dwarf party, a thing put together by a guy called David Hayles; you know, the Dwarf Party came over from Amsterdam and we picked that up in '71 and took it out on the streets of Bristol. Dave Hayles stood for election and we went around putting his manifesto through people's doors, which there was a huge outcry about because it had a four-letter word in it and silly things like that. It said about Dave Hayles: 'educated at Bristol University; has not done National Service; unmarried; acid head; interested in cannabis, rock and roll, balling and bicycles... the Dwarf movement stands for free everything: housing, medicine, love, entertainment and drugs... we feel that local government needs a fucking good shake-up on all levels ... you can contact me through your friendly neighbourhood hippy—he won't bite your head off'.
>
> Through that we got into doing our own artwork and posters, stuff from Zap Comix, that kind of thing. We had three resident artists: Pete Biles, our conga player, Kenny Wheeler the drummer and Norman Gosney, who's a cartoonist. Basically, that was how the band got started, we were sort of the house band of the Black Dwarf party.[273]

---

273 'Rustic' Rod Goodway, 'Magic Muscle #1', http://www.achingcellar.co.uk/pages/tree/magic_muscle.htm [accessed 12 August 2018]. David Hayles became a world expert on ornamental plaster and moved to New York State.

DAVE HAYLES
DWARF CABOT

This is the first time I have stood for election as one of your councillors. Councillor Bob Trevis, who has served the Cabot Ward for many years, has decided to retire.

With your support Dwarf will provide free entertainment both inside and outside the Council. We feel that local government needs a fucking good shake up at all levels.

You can contact me through your friendly neighbourhood hippy — he wont bite your head off.

Love and peace

Dave Hayles xx

dave hayles

educated at Bristol University. Has not done National service. Unmarried. Acid Head. Interested in cannabis, rock and Roll, balling and bicycles.

VOTE DWARF THIS THURSDAY

The Bristol Dwarf Party is an example of the way that some locals took up a kind of play power that explicitly referenced and aligned itself with the international counterculture. Dave 'Basil' Hayles was the sole candidate. Goodway recollects that the connection with the Dutch movement first came about when actor David Rappaport, who had achondroplasia, a form of dwarfism, came to study at the University of Bristol after spending time in Amsterdam. He had been influenced by the Provos and Kabouters while living in particularly heady days in Holland. It is likely that Rappaport would also have met poet and actor Heathcote Williams there (also linked to the Dwarfs), since the latter was living in Amsterdam at this time as one of the editors of *Suck* magazine and was thrilled by 'Provo and white bicycles and great anarchic events in the Vondelpark and marathon poetry readings in the Paradiso'.[274] Rappaport and Williams were to become Foreign Minister and Ambassador to Great Britain for the squatters' Republic of Frestonia later in the 1970s. 'Stoned negotiations' between members of Magic Muscle and Rappaport took place as they considered starting a similar movement in Bristol. This resulted in 'a couple of late-night letterbox raids around Cotham, Redlands [*sic*] & Clifton which caused a big fuss ... tripped-out & chaotic as all our ventures were'.[275]

As the 'house band' of the Dwarf Party, Magic Muscle were consciously following the role of Detroit's famous MC5, the rock-music wing of the White Panther Party, founded in support of the Black Panthers. Closer to home, the Bristol Dwarf Party's more immediate counterparts were an environmentally-minded London group called The Dwarfs which, according to Alan Dearling, made their first appearance in 1971 at the Portobello Road Carnival, 'where Hawkwind and the Pink Fairies played beneath the flyover'.[276] This clearly indicates that the West Country's Dwarfs, and those based in north London, mostly around Notting Hill,[277] both appeared in

---

Facing page—Election publicity leaflet for Dave Hayles of the Bristol Dwarf Party (1971), kindly supplied by Rod Goodway. Sadly, Dave Hayles, the Bristol Dwarf candidate, did not achieve a great breakthrough in the Council elections of May 1971, coming third with 161 votes; Labour won with 1237.

---

274 Heathcote Williams, e-mail to the author (15 January 2015).

275 'Rustic' Rod Goodway, e-mail to the author (8 October 2018).

276 Alan Dearling, 'Not Only But Also: Some Historical Ramblings About the English Festivals Scene [online] http://enablerpublications.co.uk/pdfs/notonly1.pdf [accessed 25 September 2012], 4-5.

277Andy Worthington, Stonehenge: Celebration and Subversion (Loughborough: Alternative Albion, 2004), 38.

Bristol Dwarf Party flier (1971) kindly provided by 'Rustic' Rod Goodway.

early 1971 and were close kin. The Dwarfs were also among the activist groups that blockaded London's Oxford Street in protest against traffic and consumerism in 1971.[278]

The Dwarfs in both London and Bristol had radical, utopian programmes which were in keeping with the policies of the more high-profile and moderately successful Dutch groups the Provos and their successors the Kabouters (which translates as 'dwarfs' or 'gnomes') who campaigned for civil rights, the decriminalisation of cannabis and green policies in Amsterdam and other cities in the Netherlands during the late 1960s and 1970s. Dearling also offers that it was reported in *Time Out* that London Dwarfs 'operate strictly as freak ambassadors… Dwarf power does not wish to be corrupted'.[279] A newspaper item from 1971 reports that the London Dwarfs, numbering as many as 150, launched themselves with a Carnival that attracted 3,000 and announced a manifesto whose declaration included:

> We are interested in the development of communities with healthy environments, with housing, welfare and amenities designed to give the fullest possible expression to individual and co-operative freedom.[280]

One of the main events organised by the Dwarfs in Bristol was the successful Free Festival held on Clifton Downs on 9th May 1971. This was perhaps the second free festival in the West Country and, after the Cambridge Free Festival and Phun City, one of the first of its kind in England. As such it marked the start of a free festival culture that was to flourish from the early 1970s to the early 1990s, when the last of the large DIY free festivals took place at Castlemorton.[281] Magic Muscle played alongside two other Bristol bands, Flash Gordon and Wisper, who were to become regulars at the Granary. An existing two-minute film clip of the Bristol Free Festival, featuring Flash Gordon, is a tiny portal that allows us to glimpse the event fleetingly and captures something of the spirit and vibe of this

278 Hunt, *Revolutionary Urbanism of Street Farm*, 17.
279 Dearling, 'Not Only But Also'.
280 Wallyhopes Blogspot, 'Vote Dwarf Party 71' [newspaper cutting of provenance unknown, with report by David May, from the Dial House archive (13 April 2014): http://wallyhopes.blogspot.com/2014/04/vote-dwarf-party-71.html [accessed 4 October 2018].
281 The Museum of Bath at Work exhibition 'Bonkers but Brilliant!: The Bath Arts Workshop and Bath in the 1970s' (2019) dated the city's Victoria Park Free Festival to 1970. The Criminal Justice Act (2004) effectively criminalised future free festivals like Castlemorton.

Dwarfs at Bristol Free Festival on Clifton Downs, 9 May 1971 (Photograph: Gordon Strong).

long lost spring day, nearly half a century ago.[282] The West Coast chapter of the Hells Angels, neighbours of the commune in Cotham and who minded the band equipment at the festival, also appear in the film. Dave Lawton attended the event and recalled that the Hells Angels took up the role as bodyguards, surrounding the diesel generator to stop the police and the drug squad pulling the plug.[283] A report in the national underground paper *Friends* recognised what became widely known as the 'Downs Concert' as a major event, putting the West Country firmly on the alternative map. Gordon Strong, who played at the 'Downs Concert' as frontman for Flash Gordon and who also took many photographs of the happenings on the day, comments interestingly on the event and the way that it showed and fostered the close connections between the counterculture in Bristol and London:

282 'Bristol Free Festival 1971', filmed by Bob Whitfield and edited by Gordon Strong: https://www.youtube.com/watch?v=tNApntXMN2I [accessed 22 August 2018]; Gordon Strong, 'The Bristol Free Festival 1971' http://www.ukrockfestivals.com/bristol-free-festival-1971.html [accessed 15 September 2018]
283 Dave Lawton, telephone interview with the author (16 September 2018).

You couldn't do that now. There'd be SWAT teams and tear gas. It was planned. It was planned very well. But, basically, people just turned up and did it. I mean nothing like that ever happened again. There were the Ashton Court festivals but that was a very different thing.

The fact that the Downs concert got reported in *Friends* was because of the links with the underground press in London.

Some of the London bands, people like Hawkwind, liked to come to Bristol. Because there was a scene, mainly around 49 [Cotham Brow], and they felt comfortable there. Because in a lot of those outlying places, what could they do? If they went to Taunton, who would they link up with there? There was always a bit of a scene.[284]

So, it was certainly not in the area of electoral politics, but in the development of the free festival movement that the Dwarfs were to have their largely unnoticed impact. The 1971 newspaper report on the Dwarfs of north London also featured a photograph in which the ill-fated Wally Hope (Phil Russell) appears as a prominent member of the group. Wally Hope, along with Heathcote Williams and others, was to become one of the self-styled Wallies of Wessex, and was the inspiration for, and founder of, the Stonehenge People's Free Festival. From the first gathering in 1974, Stonehenge was to become the West Country's largest and longest lasting free festival before police attacked the travellers setting up the event during the notorious Battle of the Beanfield in 1985. Of the first Stonehenge gathering, Heathcote Williams wrote:

I was at Stonehenge after Windsor. It's a bit of a blur as everyone was pretty bruised.

There was also a confrontation between Phil [Wally Hope] and Ubi [Dwyer]. Phil was all for a strategic withdrawal to Stonehenge and

284 Gordon Strong, interview with the author (La Ruca Café, Gloucester Road, Bristol 28 February 2019). The photograph below features Norman Gosney. ukrockfestivals.com homepage, 'The Bristol Free Festival 1971', photograph of Bristol Dwarfs by Gordon Strong: http://www.ukrockfestivals.com/bristol-free-festival-1971.html [accessed 18 January 2019]. The gay liberation poster is being held by Gosney, who left Bristol for New York where he took up residence in the penthouse and the Bristol Gardens, on top of the world-famous Chelsea Hotel for the next twenty-five years. He developed a business empire as a nightclub operator before relocating to Shanghai where he also started up a burlesque and performance club before eventually returning to live in London: https://www.normangosney.co.uk/about.html [accessed 3 March 2019].

Ubi had been arrested (for attacking a fire engine that had entered the Windsor site—a somewhat misplaced target, and he'd also clearly lost the plot since he (Ubi/Bill) was now declaring himself the rightful heir to the UK throne—hence reason got the better of me and I joined forces with Phil and at his invitation went down to Stonehenge which he insisted was going to be the new Eden.

As you will know yourself a bendy made out of black plastic bags on a windswept MOD plain is not Club Med, but Hawkwind and Wally's zest for life made up for a lot.[285]

Wally Hope died in mysterious circumstances in 1975.[286] By the 1980s, surrealist dwarfs also emerged in Poland's Orange Alternative to mock Wojciech Jaruzelski's authoritarian government. In the present day, something of the spirit of the dwarf movements continues in the form of the libertarian International Pirate Party which promotes direct democracy and civil rights.

Other voices: Bristol's alternative media

Alternative media spanned the artistic and political wings of the counterculture. Given the thriving alternative society and the presence of a University in the area, it is unsurprising that radical media was published and distributed locally. The advent of offset lithography began to make local press production more accessible and affordable during the 1960s. By the late 1960s and early 1970s, radical news-sheets not only reflected the existence of the counterculture, but also stimulated its ideas and development. The pioneering London-based *International Times* was keen to include regional coverage, so gigs and other events in the West Country regularly appeared in its listings. Although some home-grown papers were produced in Bristol, copies of obscure ephemeral titles with tiny print runs are now extremely rare, if indeed any have survived at all. An early example is *Sixty-Five*, published by radical students at the University of Bristol. University students also produced at least two radical bulletins, *Open Conspiracy* and *Offensive* during and in the aftermath of the occupations of late 1968. By 1969, the Bristol Arts Lab, part of the South-West Arts Lab Co-op, was producing *Cough (Up Your Thing)* and a poetry magazine

285 Heathcote Williams, e-mail to the author (17 February 2011).
286 Circumstances which are set out in detail by his friend, Penny Rimbaud in *The Last of the Hippies: An Hysterical Romance* [1982] (London: Active Distribution, 2009) and *Shibboleth: My Revolting Life* (Edinburgh: AK Press with Exitstencil Press, 1998).

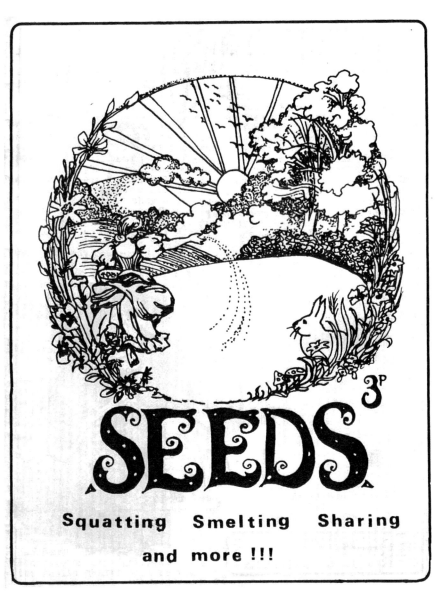

Front cover of *Seeds*: Bristol's Street Press (1971).

called *Imprint*, with a contact address at 50 Archfield Road, Cotham,[287] and were also involved with putting together *Endgine,* a news-sheet for Bristol and the West Country, with 8 Southernhay Crescent, Cliftonwood as its contact address.[288] More specialised was *Transmit*, published by, and to promote, the Bristol Free Radio Movement from 1969 to 1972.[289]

In 1970, Bristol finally gained its own 'underground' paper when *Seeds: Bristol's Street Press*, appeared in Clifton and ran for four issues until 1971. Published at what is now the Youth Education Service[290] premises at 14 Frederick Place, it set out its purpose as follows:

> We hope to give voice to the discontent that is rising over unemployment, bad housing, the Outer Circuit Road, unscrupulous property speculation and others. *Seeds* is intended to be a forum for constructive radical activity, to provide information, and act as a clearing house for ideas.[291]

Issue three had a print run of 1500 copies. Reports included the new multiple squats in Park Place and the enthusiastic encounter with 'underground theatre group' the Crystal Theatre of the Saint cited above. *Seeds* 4 attacked the profiteering of new-age groups who were turning spiritual growth into a commodity and 'hip capitalism', showing itself to be consistently vigilant when it came to the commercialisation and appropriation of the counterculture. These anti-capitalist instincts show that local members of the counterculture were sharply aware of the critical distinction between a progressive, community-oriented, social justice agenda and those whose aspirations were limited to considerations of profit-making to support individualistic motivations to enjoy a groovy lifestyle. Following the principle of providing information for action, *Seeds* also included a useful directory of

287 See *International Times* 1.66 (October 1969). See *International Times Archive:* http://www.internationaltimes.it/archive/page.php?i=IT_1969-10-10_B-IT-Volume-1_Iss-66_016&view=text

288 See *International Times* 1.67 (November 1969). In *International Times Archive:* http://www.internationaltimes.it/archive/page.php?i=IT_1969-11-06_B-IT-Volume-1_Iss-67_016&view=text

289 See *International Times* 1.79 (May 1970). See *International Times Archive:* http://www.internationaltimes.it/archive/page.php?i=IT_1970-05-08_B-IT-Volume-1_Iss-79_024&view=text . Bristol Free Radio Movement seems to have been a short-lived venture, active around 1969 to 1970, with meetings in Westbury-on-Trym and contact addresses in Cotham Lawn Road and in Kingswood.

290 Then shared with Bristol School Leavers' Project.

291 John Spiers, *The Underground and Alternative Press in England: A Bibliographical Guide with Historical Notes* (Hassocks: Harvester Press, 1974), 49.

INSIDE:

HOME GRANTS: Too Poor To Improve? Page 3.
MOTORWAY: Dividing The Community. Page 6.
EDUCATION: Facts That Concern You. Centre Pages.
LETTERS: Readers chance to write. Page 2.

ST WERBURGHS   ST PAULS   MONTPELIER   EASTON   NO.2   PRICE 2p

Front cover of *SPAM* no. 2 (1972).

Top—'It's a great area…so uplifting!!', *SPAM* (1972). Middle—'I understand he's from the Planning Department', *SPAM* (1974). Bottom—'Who Rules Bristol?... Homes not profits… Down with offices' *Tenants' News* (1974).

alternative Bristol, with entries including such Clifton-based radical bastions as the Women's Liberation Group, the Bristol Libertarian Group, the Brook Advisory Centre (for accessible birth control) and the Bristol Claimants' Union. In this way the paper strived to provide a platform for dissident voices, bring about greater cohesion within the counterculture by networking, and positively promoting the infrastructure of the alternative society.

Of these, the Women's Liberation Group was to develop significantly over the coming years producing their own newsletter called *Enough* from 1970 onwards. *Enough* is believed to have had a circulation of 500 at its peak.[292] *Enough* was joined by *The Gay Women's Newsletter,* soon retitled *Move* and published by Bristol Gay Women's Group, also based at the Women's Centre. We will meet Bristol's second- wave feminists shortly.

Another radical newspaper serving Bristol in the early 1970s was *SPAM*, a community paper started in St Werburghs in 1972. *SPAM*, reporting on issues in the wards of St Werburghs, St Pauls, Montpelier and Easton, had a strong class analysis from the start, often drawing stark comparisons with the wealthier neighbourhood of Clifton: The opening editorial for the first edition:

If our area disappeared many city services would grind to a halt [...] Conditions which would not be allowed to persist for five minutes in Clifton are O.K. for us. It is we who subsidise prosperous suburbia, not the other way round.[293]

In the same edition, David Hirschman forcefully argued against the Outer Circuit Road which would cut across St Pauls:

Alderman Gervase Walker, Chairman of the Planning Committee, said it was 'unthinkable' to put an urban motorway through Cotham and Clifton. It should be underground. But if it is unthinkable in these districts, why is it not unthinkable in Saint Pauls and Montpelier? Possibly because people in Clifton will resist any attempt to devastate their homes effectively. So people here must show that it is unthinkable to drive an urban motorway through the heart of their community too.[294]

292 Figure from Sistershow Revisited blog (29 October 2010): https://sistershowrevisited. wordpress.com/page/8/ [accessed 20 November 2011].
293 [Anon.], 'Editorial: A Problem Area", *SPAM*, no .1 [1972], 1 and 8.
294 David Hirschman, 'Motorway Madness—Saint Pauls Style?', *SPAM*, no .1 [1972], 4.

Also concerned with the built environment, the launch of a monthly news-sheet called *Tenants' News* in 1973 was particularly relevant to the changing situation in Clifton. The Clifton Tenants' Association (CTA) was set up to focus on housing problems, with an address at 27 Royal York Crescent. Carter's inclusion of evictions in *Shadow Dance* suggests that the precarious nature of working-class accommodation was already apparent in the Clifton and Hotwells area and pointed to the potential for greater insecurity of tenure in the coming years and decades. This had proved prescient. In the early 1970s, homelessness re-emerged as a leading issue, to be dramatically exacerbated during the 1980s and 1990s and reaching epidemic proportions since.[295] This housing crisis has been characterised by a shift in the profile of homelessness, with increasing numbers of young single people becoming homeless in Bristol and nationally since the 1970s, despite the significant increase in society's productive capacity during the interim. During the early 1970s the crescents and terraces of Clifton became a focus for housing activism since it was populated by tenants who were willing to organise to protect affordable housing.

The CTA was formed to confront the systemic failure to provide decent accommodation for all. The group organised to take collective action on local issues, holding that 'tenants' rights and interests can only be fully protected and advanced by the combined experience and energy of an organisation and not by individuals acting alone'.[296] *Tenants' News* supported tenants in their struggles against landlords and for the construction of affordable housing rather than office blocks, printing exposés about property speculation in the city. The news-sheet also provided updates on squatters' activism in the area, and had links to the Bristol Squatters' Union, based at 16 Osborne Villas, Cotham.

In 1974 the CTA sympathised with the temporary occupation of Henry Hyam's Centre Point (built in London in 1963) to draw attention to property speculation:

Centre Point was occupied because it has become the concrete symbol of everything that is rotten in our unequal society. More than a quarter of a million square feet of empty offices, built for profit, kept empty for profit.[297]

295 Suzanne Fitzpatrick, Peter Kemp and Suzanne Klinker, *Single Homelessness: An Overview of Research in Britain* (Bristol: Policy Press, 2000), 4-5: https://www.jrf.org.uk/report/single-homelessness-overview-research-britain [accessed 12 November 2018].
296 Clifton Tenants' Association, 'Where we stand', *Tenants' News* Special no, 9 (1974), 10.
297 Clifton Tenants' Association statement (21 January 1974), Stop press pull-out in *Tenants' News* 3 (January/February 1974).

Architects Summer Tour: "Wow! That must be more than 30 million square feet of office space out there!", *Tenants' News* (1974).

"Well they wanted some housing as well", *Tenants' News* (1974)

This was symbolic of a situation that the Clifton housing activists recognised locally, where office blocks were being constructed on prime land in the city centre. More than forty years later, this practice is familiar to present-day groups such as Abolish Empty Office Buildings,[298] who are working to highlight the issue and starting up projects to address the problem.

In recent years more atomised, demoralised and traumatised urban communities have been less able to organise and resist. Nevertheless, Bristol is a stronghold for grassroots activists in the housing union Acorn which is organising to fight evictions and campaigning for better conditions in the rented sector.[299]

1975 saw the launch of the *Bristol Voice*, a regular and comprehensive title which became the city's longest-running alternative paper of the late twentieth century, producing well over 50 issues before it ceased in 1981. Produced by Bristol Cooperative Press, the non-aligned *Bristol Voice* was an agit-prop community paper that reported upon and inspired activism for social justice and environmental causes, with extensive listings and coverage on core issues such as housing, health and social care, industrial struggles and education. It was a significant forerunner of more mainstream listings magazines such as *Out West* and *Venue*, as well as later trouble-making publications such as *The Bristolian* 'smiting the high and mighty' since 2001, the defunct *Bristle* and the more recent independent community paper *The Bristol Cable*, launched in 2014.[300]

Early Women's Liberation in Bristol

The Bristol Women's Liberation Group was not only a pioneering group regionally, but its contributions and campaigning energy were to become a catalyst for the emergence of second-wave feminism nationally. Locally, the movement began in May 1969 when Ellen Malos and Lee Cataldi hosted the first meetings of the Bristol Women's Group.[301] The Bristol group were, therefore, already active before the famous inaugural Women's Liberation Movement Conference at Ruskin College in Oxford in 1970, an event to

298 See Abolish Empty Office Blocks website: https://www.aeobhousepeople.org.uk/ [accessed 12 November 2018].
299 See Acorn website: https://acorntheunion.org.uk/ [accessed 12 November 2018].
300 Ongoing titles available from: https://thebristolian.net/ and https://thebristolcable.org/ .
301 *Sistershow Revisited: Feminism in Bristol 1973-1975*, collected by Deborah M. Withers ([Bristol] HammerOn Press, 2011), 19.

which its activists contributed.[302] In July 1973 Bristol hosted the 5th National Women's Liberation Movement Conference in the University of Bristol Students' Union building, in Queens Road, Clifton.[303] The Bristol group's early core members, Ellen Malos, Lee Cataldi, Janet Parham, Beverly Skinner, Carole Dark, Monica Sjöö, Pat VT West, were either residents of Clifton or the neighbouring districts of Redland and Cotham. Swedish artist and activist Monica Sjöö had first moved to Bristol in 1957, while poet and performance artist Pat VT West (1938-2008) had arrived in 1967.[304] The original members of the Bristol Women's Liberation group came from divergent backgrounds, prompting Pat VT West to recall that a 'two-pronged way' soon emerged, given that meetings were held alternately between the basement flat of the Malos family, whom she considered to be 'left-wing middle-class academics' and the contrasting home of Beverly Skinner (1938-1999).[305] Skinner, later described in the *Evening Post* as 'one of Bristol's most controversial artists in the 1970s'[306] was equally left-wing, yet increasingly inhabited the outer-reaches of dissident thought, placing her hopes in cosmic spiritual transformation rather than class struggle. 1970 was the year that she also began 'The Book of Paradise on Earth' an esoteric manuscript channelled during dream states that she was to work on for the remaining three decades of her life. Such difference was a foretaste of the divergence of the women's movement and the wider counterculture, which fractured into diverse political and spiritual programmes which were rarely integrated and often incompatible.

The creation of the Bristol Women's Centre in 1973, initially accommodated in Ellen Malos's basement, consolidated the achievements of the local women's group when they secured more outward facing premises in 1979. This extended

302 Feminist Archive South, Personal Histories of the Second Wave of Feminism summarised from interviews by Viv Honeybourne and Ilona Singer (Volumes One and Two), interview with Ellen Malos, 24-25: http://feministarchivesouth.org.uk/wp-content/uploads/2013/02/Personal-Histories-of-the-Second-Wave-of-Feminism.pdf [accessed 19 July 2018]. See *International Times* 1.72 (January 1970). See *International Times Archive:* http://www.internationaltimes.it/archive/page.php?i=IT_1970-01-28_B-IT-Volume-1_Iss-72_028&view=text

303 Withers, *Sistershow Revisited*, 64-67.

304 Pat VT West, 'Monica Sjoo: Artist, Writer, Activist, Visionary', Eulogy delivered at funeral ceremony (August 2005), [online] www.monicasjoo.org [accessed via Internet Archive Wayback Machine 28 September 2018].

305 University of Bristol Special Collections Archive: Pat V T West Papers: DM2123/1/ Archive Box 92 File 2 (Beverly Skinner), Pat V T West, 'Beverly: "The Daughter of the English Renaissance"' (September 1999).

306 The manuscript was to cause upset when Skinner's son, Cameron, donated the manuscript to the Bristol Theosophical Society at the end of his mother's life when she died in1999, only for it to be returned later on the grounds that it was believed to be 'haunted'. See 'Chilling Tale of Artist's Words with an X Factor', *Evening Post* (26 October 1999).

the impact they could have in terms of promotion of their cause and practical services. Angela Rodaway who was instrumental in setting up the Women's Centre had been at the forefront of the Women's Abortion and Contraception Campaign.[307] Jane Duffus records that Rodaway was to continue to campaign for social justice and women's causes, whether economic, cultural or spiritual, from her basement flat in Windsor Terrace, Clifton, for the rest of her long life.[308] As we have seen, several of the original members of the Bristol Women's Liberation Group and Angela Rodaway launched the celebrated experiment in alternative theatre, Sistershow, as a fund-raiser for the Centre. Sistershow was to provide the entertainment for the national Women's Liberation conference when it was hosted at the University of Bristol in July 1973.

The extent of Angela Carter's connections with Bristol's women's liberationists before she left the city in 1969 is unknown. She is, however, recorded as sharing a platform with Monica Sjöö during a panel discussion on 'Politics and the Arts' on a return visit to Bristol in 1978.[309] A debate between Carter and Sjöö would have been fascinating. As a tireless activist and artist, it would be difficult to imagine a more archetypal countercultural figure than Sjöö, since she participated in activities that came to define the radical alternative society. She campaigned against the Vietnam War, supported the student occupations of 1968, networked with other anarchists internationally, including King Mob, Phil Cohen, Murray and Bea Bookchin and Ben Morea of the 'Up Against the Wall Motherfuckers' group, was bisexual and a passionate supporter of women's and gay liberation, experimented with psychedelic drugs, lived in a communal squat at 11 Durdham Park, Bristol from 1978 to 1980 and shifted her campaigning energies to the Greenham Common anti-nuclear protests in the 1980s. As an artist, she was also definitive and provocative. An early exhibition at St Ives featuring a (female) 'God giving birth' was banned when an art culture that routinely displayed female nudity ironically found a portrait of childbirth as an act of creation too controversial. Sjöö's powerful imagery, inspired by archaeological representations of women, was to become definitive of the art of Goddess spirituality and neo-paganism. Fellow Clifton artist Bob Gale described her in short as 'a formidable woman'.[310] In early 2004 I attended what would be one of Sjöö's final public talks at an exhibition at

307 Withers, *Sistershow Revisited*, 69.
308 Jane Duffus, *The Women Who Built Bristol 1184-2018* (Bristol: Tangent, 2018), 298-99. Rodaway was also, along with Paul Stephenson (celebrated for his role in the Bristol Bus Boycott), a founder member of Bristol's Campaign Against Racial Discrimination in 1967—see White, *Monica Sjöö: Life and Letters*, 39.
309 An event organised by the local Communist Party, according to White, *Monica Sjöö: Life and Letters*, 100.
310 Bob Gale, telephone interview with the author (26 November 2018).

Top left—'WILD TREE-WOMAN' by Beverly Skinner (1978).

Top right—'A DOVE NEAR A FIG TREE, BRISTOL, ENGLAND, 1969' by Beverly Skinner.

Middle right—Photograph of Beverly Skinner (c1970): 'MAKING THE PARADISE ON EARTH IS THE BEST SOLUTION, FOR MORTALS AND IMMORTALS'. Skinner wrote in block capitals.

Bottom—'A SUNDAY AFTERNOON WALK, IN BRISTOL AT ASHTON COURT PARK' (1968) by Beverly Skinner.

Early issues of *Enough: The Journal of the Bristol Women's Liberation Group*, first published in 1970.

The Journal of the Bristol Women's Liberation group

Statement by Bristol feminist artists Monica Sjöö, Liz Moore and Ann Berg, marked Bristol 30 May 1972.

Bath's Hotwells Gallery. I wrote a review for *Bristle* magazine which included the following:

> Monica Sjöö treated people who turned up on Saturday to slide-show chats in which she explained how she felt like a medium for the symbolic imagery of her art and described the trance-like states of emotion in which it is created. As we sat back and listened it became evident that the paintings were always produced with a sense of wonder, that they frequently expressed much pain but were also often created with more than a twinkle of mischief. Sjöö's presence is as enchanting as her art and despite her illness, her life force remains undiminished.[311]

I would speculate that, while Carter is likely to have diverged from some of the aspects of Goddess worship that Sjöö embraced, the two contrarians would have shared scepticism towards capitalism and that Carter would have been in sympathy with Sjöö's robust opposition to right-wing elements within new ageism.

'Pushing at the Frontiers of Everything': The 1970s Counterculture in Bath

Angela Carter left Bristol in 1969 to go for an extended stay in Japan during which she resolved to end her marriage to Paul Carter. She kept in contact with friends in Bristol during the early 1970s and was to return to the city regularly during the remainder of her life. Dave Lawton remembered bumping into the novelist many years later at a street fair in Kingsdown. This chance encounter in Bristol during the early 1990s was to be the last time he saw his friend, since it seems she was already suffering from the onset of the terminal illness that was to end her relatively short life.[312]

In 1973, after living in Japan and divorcing Paul Carter, Angela Carter returned to the West Country, this time to live in Bath. After relocating to Bath in April 1973,[313] she briefly lodged with their mutual friend Edward

311 [Anon.], 'Trance-formation: Monica Sjoo at the Temple of Sulis', *Bristle* 16 (Spring/Summer 2004), 34.
312 Dave Lawton, telephone interview with the author (18 January 2018).
313 There are discrepancies between two major sources for the dates that Carter lived in Bath. Gordon dates Carter's move to stay with Horesh in Bath to 1973, and her departure from the city to move to Clapham to 1976 in *Invention of Angela Carter*, 222 and 265; Frayling cites the date of her move to Bath as 1972 and from Bath as 1977 in *Inside the Bloody Chamber*, 16 and 39.

Horesh, before moving into 5 Hay Hill where she lived until returning to London in 1976. During the 1970s and 1980s, Georgian Bath had shed much of the pomposity and formality of its heyday to become an easy-going city, with lively street life and a flourishing alternative scene. In her 1975 article 'Bath: A Heritage City', first published in *New Society*, Carter struggled to reconcile the city's contradictions in her mind but captured them perfectly, concluding that 'Bath, in its romantic, dishevelled loveliness, is no longer the city the Woods built'.[314] During Carter's years in the city, the Georgian splendour was shared between residents of the privileged and respectable kind, an expanding student population following the development of the University of Bath during the mid-1960s, an established counterculture, mostly centred around the Walcot district, a working-class population concentrated around the periphery in areas such as Oldfield Park, Twerton and Whiteway and many visitors. In 1975 Nicholas Saunders described the city as follows in *Alternative England and Wales*:

> Bath is basically a classy conservative town, but has become what Notting Hill once was, though with more gays and practically no blacks. Being the 'scene place', it has attracted people from all over the country, many of them young and some very untogether.[315]

In 1974 actor Robert Llewellyn was told 'You gotta go to Bath man, it's really cool'.[316] So he did. Bath had become an increasingly significant draw within the cosmos of the alternative society as the 1970s progressed. Influenced by the American beats as well as English radical traditions, poets Dennis Gould and Pat VT West had organised an anarchist poetry festival in the city centre as early as 1965. Around 1967-1968 Roy Emery and Geoff Barfoot were producing an anarchist-oriented 'propaganda-sheet' called *Scrump* in Bath.[317] Pre-dating Woodstock by two months, 1969 saw the first Bath Festival of the Blues, held at the Bath Recreation Ground on 28th June 1969, featuring leading bands such as Led Zeppelin, Fleetwood Mac, John Mayall's Bluesbreakers, Ten Years After and The Nice. The following year an even mightier event was staged at nearby Shepton Mallet, headlined by

314 Angela Carter, 'Bath, Heritage City' [1975], 71-76 in *Nothing Sacred: Selected Writings* (London: Virago, 1982), 75.
315 Saunders *et al.*, *Alternative England and Wales*, 16. While Bath was less diverse than Notting Hill or neighbouring Bristol, there were more established ethnic minority communities in the city than this suggests.
316 Robert Llewellyn at The Past, Present and Future of Community Energy event, Museum of Bath at Work (15 June 2019).
317 *Freedom* (20 June 2009), 11.

Looking down Hay Hill from Lansdown Road towards The Paragon (top). 5 Hay Hill, Bath, where Angela Carter lived from 1973-1976 (bottom).

'a' group activities ···
the octagon june·11·12·
milsom st· bath 8·p·m·

Ticket for anarchist poetry performance in Bath organised by Dennis Gould and Pat VT West in 1965.

legendary rock acts including Jefferson Airplane, Pink Floyd and Led Zeppelin and attracting upwards of 150,000 people. Such events put Bath and the West Country on the map as a foremost destination for the alternative society. This was enhanced by the appearance and development of the Bath Arts Workshop in the late 1960s and 1970s.

Like Clifton in the 1960s, the central wards of Bath were more affordable during the 1970s than in the present day. One local factor was a plan for a major road which would cut through the city centre to make way for increasing numbers of cars. This proposal threatened swathes of Bath with demolition, while blighting other neighbourhoods with uncertainty. Adam Fergusson, whose melancholy yet forcefully argued and influential book *The Sack of Bath* helped to prevent further destruction, wrote in 1973 that 'almost every construction for 20 years in Bath has to some degree been an environmental calamity, a few less catastrophic than others but not one a positive embellishment to the City'.[318] There were two significant consequences of this impending development. First, increases in property prices and rent in affected areas were curbed. Second, the destruction provoked organised resistance from activists opposed to the road on conservation and environmental grounds. These factors opened a space for experimentation and for progressive initiatives to emerge.

Hay Hill is adjacent to The Paragon which forms one edge of Walcot. Christopher Frayling's book *Inside the Bloody Chamber* (2015) is an excellent personal and academic account of his friendship with Angela Carter and her literary output during her years in Bath. Frayling speaks of unofficial aspirations at the time for Walcot to be 'a kind of nascent Left Bank' and Carter's love for the:

318 Adam Fergusson, *The Sack of Bath: A Record and an Indictment* (Salisbury: Compton Russell, 1973), 16.

'*other* beautiful people', not wealthy celebrities but the counter-cultural characters that she met, the squatters who lived next door and many others including 'the earnest arts workshop organisers, the craftspeople, the tattooists, the street marketeers, the flute-players, the émigrés from Notting Hill, the performers and exhibitors in Walcot Village Hall…. and the people who put notices in the health-food shop offering their organic garbage free to any needy goat'.[319]

Shepherd's purse, Bilbo's Bookshop, the Brillig Art Centre, the Alternative Bookshop, Tumi, Arcania, the Broad Street Bakery, the Walrus and Carpenter, Aspidistra were among Bath's independent shops; their names, taken from the realms of nonsense and fantasy, form something of a poetic litany. The Hat and Feather, the pub and music venue at the top of Walcot Street, was the capital of Walcot bohemia, with its interior of acid-Victoriana. Further out towards the Wiltshire border were the Green Lantern Café and the Mead Tea Gardens.

Harvest Wholefoods was a short walk from Carter's front door, the unnamed subject of 'The New Vegetarians' (1976), an article written for *New Society*. This workers' cooperative has been in Walcot, the heart of alternative Bath, since it was founded in 1971. It now stands with The Bell, another of Angela Carter's favourite haunts in the 1970s, as a remnant of Walcot's more bohemian days, following the loss of such old favourites as The Hat and Feather, The Beehive and Walcot Reclamation, and the branding of Walcot Street as the 'Artisans' Quarter'. In *Alternative England and Wales* for 1975, Harvest, described as 'the best wholefood shop in the country outside London' is listed as still being located at 31 Belvedere, Lansdown Road (close to Hay Hill).[320] Carter commended and gently satirised the wholefood suppliers in 'The New Vegetarians', which was published in 1976, a time when it was still possible to label vegetarianism as a 'food fetish' and before expressing some moral objections to its moral objections and offering some counterpoints of the vegetables-feel-pain-too variety.[321] Nevertheless, while the fashion for macrobiotic diets has been and gone since the 1970s, lacto-vegetarianism and veganism have rocketed and mushroomed. Macrobiotics are also listed among the eccentrics that Carter listed in 'Bath: A Heritage City' (1975).[322]

319 Frayling, *Inside the Bloody Chamber*, 18.
320 Saunders *et al.*, *Alternative England and Wales*, 16 and 75.
321 An idea to which Carter hilariously returns later in her final novel *Wise Children* (London: Vintage, 1992), 91.
322 Carter, 'Bath, Heritage City', 72.

Walcot was also the home of the Bath Arts Workshop, founded in 1969 by Phil Shepherd and Rick Knapp. This group was to become one of the most active and impactful of the groups linked to the art labs movement outside of London. By the mid-1970s the Bath Arts Workshop had merged into a loose network of community projects working collectively and initiating an impressive number of independent services that were free or low-cost. Among the many offshoots of the Bath Arts Workshop, the Natural Theatre Company (now looning around internationally) and the Walcot festivals were to make a tangible impression on the city and far beyond, while Comtek, the Community Technology Centre was to have a national impact. John's Bikes (business closed in November 2018) provided affordable bikes and repair, yards for building materials and timber (eventually to become Walcot Reclamation) supplied cheap re-purposed artefacts and materials for restoration, Bath Community Video, together with several art studios and projects attracted creative workers and designers, while others worked on gardening and food production. Regularly printed newsletters such as the *Workshop Manual* and fliers shared information about news, events and services while The Hat and Feather and Auntie Margaret's Café in The Paragon were important community venues closely linked to the Bath Arts Workshop.

At a time when people were upgrading their televisions from black and white to colour, the spirit of festivity brought by the Bath Arts Workshop added colour and sound to the streets of Walcot. Local hotelier and entrepreneur Charlie Ware funded many Bath Arts Workshop events from the early 1970s onwards. Ware recycled profits from his business, the luxurious Cleveland Hotel in Great Pulteney Street, to support community projects and to sponsor concerts at the Bath Theatre Royal.[323] Architectural artist Glyn Davies, who moved to Bath in 1972, described the highlights of an alternative festival that was centred on the Cleveland Hotel. The event took place over ten days in May-June 1972 and featured the creation of 'an amazing upside down room' in the Hotel and included a set by the Global Village Trucking Company which was sustained non-stop for hours as members of the band, organised as a collective, dropped in and out.[324] Angela Carter's friends, performance artists Shirley Cameron and Roland Miller also visited Bath when these happenings were taking place. Cameron remembers the occasion as an extraordinary, one-off, unrepeatable experience with all the fixtures and fittings of the Hotel, down

323 Glyn Davies, personal conversation with the author (Upper Swainswick, 17 July 2016).
324 Glyn Davies, personal conversation with the author (Upper Swainswick, 17 July 2016). Other commentators have shared their memories of the early Bath free festivals online, adding dependable festival favourites Hawkwind and Magic Muscle to the list of bands that performed. See UK Rock Festivals website, 'Bath Free festivals. 1972-1979. Widcombe Manor and other venues': http://www.ukrockfestivals.com/bath-free-fest-72.html [accessed 29 January 2019].

to crockery and cutlery, being available for use by the festival goers.[325] Miller, veteran of mid-1960s underground troupe, The People Show, contributed alternative performances to further liven the celebration in Great Pulteney Street.[326] Cameron and Miller also supported a guest appearance by renowned beat poet Allen Ginsberg at the follow-up event dubbed 'Another Festival', where they did a piece called 'Other Performances' in 1973. They recalled that he seemed rather bemused as they performed around him, perhaps detracting attention from him in their scantily clad state on stage at Bath Theatre Royal.[327]

Bath retained its status as a centre for offbeat arts, music and street performance over the decades to come. In 1976, the wealthy American educationist, artist and environmental sponsor Karl Jaeger opened the Wonderland-themed Brillig Arts Centre, in New Bond Street, at the southern approaches to Walcot. The Brillig was closely connected to the Bath Arts Workshop and was an early venue for the seminal Bath Fringe Festival. Alongside steaming teas and coffees the Brillig hosted art exhibitions and over the years served up such eclectic musical fare as performances by the likes of prog rockers Henry Cow and Red Balune, acid-folk godfather Robin Williamson and new wave band The Zones. *Alternative England and Wales* cited the Bath Arts Workshop as 'both the cause and the result of most activities—besides providing information and helping people in various ways they organise events'.[328] Based in London Road, the *Bath Spark* was launched as a community paper in 1978 to report upon Bath's alternative society and the city's wider radical politics and culture.[329] One of the most colourful and enduring groups that emerged from the Walcot 'scene' was the Natural Theatre Company, still based in Bath and thriving after nearly half a century. The Natural Theatre Company grew directly out of the Bath Arts Workshop (and is still registered as the Bath Arts Workshop).

Angela Carter gravitated towards the performance artists working within the Bath Arts Workshop and met friends and collaborators Shirley Cameron and Roland Miller during her years in Bath in the mid-1970s. Although they

325 Shirley Cameron and Roland Miller personal conversation with the author (Sheffield, 25 January 2019).

326 Shirley Cameron, telephone interview with the author (8 November 2018).

327 Shirley Cameron and Roland Miller personal conversation with the author (Sheffield, 25 January 2019).

328 Saunders *et al.*, *Alternative England and Wales*, 16.

329 Steve Poole, '"A community paper means something different to everybody": The early years of *Bath Spark*', *Recovering the Regional Radical Press in Britain 1968-88* website (6 March 2019): https://radpresshistory.wordpress.com/2019/03/06/a-community-newspaper-means-something-different-to-everybody-the-early-years-of-bath-spark/#more-138 [accessed 13 June 2019].

lived in Swansea, Shirley Cameron and Roland Miller had a longstanding working relationship with other Bath Arts Workshop members, participating as part of the group during Bath Fringe events throughout the 1970s. In 1971, they created, with Bath Arts Workshop, the Cyclamen Cyclists who would cycle around Swansea dressed entirely in dark pink cyclamen clothes and stop in various locations to give impromptu performances. More performance art would follow in Bath. 'Insiders' took place over a week in Walcot Village Hall in 1974. During this time visitors were invited to step into a staging of everyday life, which continued within a netted space in Walcot Village Hall. Shirley Cameron and Roland Miller looked after their twin babies, alongside the impedimenta of daily existence, all of whom were confined inside this installation. Roger Perry (1944-1991), photographer of experimental theatre, captured the spectacle beautifully. 1975 saw the production of Red Line, a further installation in Walcot Village Hall, and 'Spotted Window', in which the artists appeared/disappeared camouflaged in spotted outfits against a spotted background to the bemusement of pedestrians walking past the window front of the Bath Arts Workshop building in Walcot Street.

Shirley Cameron recalls 'searching out' Angela Carter and first visiting the novelist at Hay Hill during the mid-1970s. They arrived with their baby twins who were quite noisy at the time, prompting them to joke that that 'they come in stereo'.[330] Angela Carter, Shirley Cameron and Roland Miller quickly found common ground, establishing a firm friendship, and they began to collaborate on fresh projects. Carter wrote the script for a new work of experimental theatre called *Ceremonies and Transformations of the Beasts*. Roland Miller, Shirley Cameron and Miguel Yeco (a Portuguese artist) performed the piece at Walcot Village Hall as part of Bath Fringe Festival in 1977. Cameron wore a giant papier-mâché beast's head, lizard-like scales and body art as she metamorphosised across species-barriers. Unfortunately, the script for this work does not seem to have survived. *Ceremonies and Transformations of the*

Facing page:
Top left—Shirley Cameron and Roland Miller, 'Insides', Walcot Village Hall, Bath (1974).
Top right—Exhibition artwork by Roland Miller (top of page: 'a series of "self-portraits taken from performances"') and Shirley Cameron, drawn in 1975, when they were working closely with the Bath Arts Workshop. Roland Miller's caption reads: 'Post- industrial/political revolutionary Europe is our inheritance – only as free individuals can we show how to cheat the exploiters'.
Bottom—Shirley Cameron and Roland Miller, 'Spotted Window', Bath Arts Workshop shop, Walcot Street, Bath (1975).

---

330 Shirley Cameron, telephone interview with the author (8 November 2018).

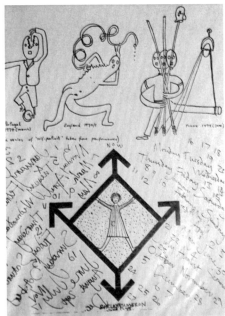

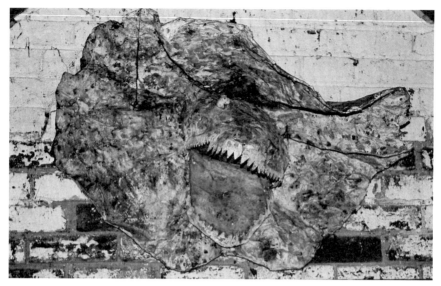

The author photographed this papier-mâché beast's head in Shirley Cameron and Roland Miller's garage at their home in Sheffield. It appeared more than forty years earlier in Walcot, Bath, as part of a performance of *Ceremonies and Transformations of the Beasts*, a play with a script written by Angela Carter in 1977.

Beasts is believed to have been a prototype for some of the transformatory creatures among the bestiary that would inhabit *The Bloody Chamber*, Carter's famous short story collection. This work in Bath was the start of a fruitful collaboration as they continued to work together in Portugal and Wales over the following decade. Also in 1977, Carter travelled to an international festival in Caldas da Rainha in Portugal with Cameron and Miller where she reported upon several of their performances. These included 'Washing the Twins', in which Carter participated in a role that involved scrubbing a statute while Shirley Cameron washed her young daughters, Lois and Collette. The next collaborative project was the more extensive *Noughts & Crosses— The History of Western Civilisation*, work created for a month-long artistic residency in Chapter Arts Centre, Cardiff in 1979. Carter's contribution to the accompanying exhibition included a document entitled 'There's no Such Thing as a Free Lunch'. This continued her preoccupation with the properties of transformation, this time in the culinary realm, reflecting her longstanding interest in the culture of food, a common theme both in Carter's fiction and non-fiction:

The cooks, like priests, preside over fire and alchemic transmutations, the waiters distribute the sacrament of FOOD in full view of those majestic symbols of our culture with which we have surrounded you.[331]

So locally, the Bath Arts Workshop occupied an appreciable part of the physical and cultural space opened up in part due to the possibilities created by low rent. Glyn Davies' excellent illustration of the diverse yet mutually supporting infrastructure of the Bath Arts Workshop (see below), drawn in February 1976, is similar to Clifford Harper's celebrated illustrations, such as the 'autonomous terrace', drawn for *Radical Technology*, a compendium of alternative living published in the same year.[332] With their complementary depictions of solidly integrated collective schemes, visionary yet practical, Davies' and Harper's meticulously detailed drawings have much in common, although were done entirely independently. There is, however, an important distinction to be made. While Harper's drawing is loosely based upon initiatives in the squatted areas of Kentish Town and Camden that existed at the time, it is proposed as a 'vision', largely an imagined utopia. By contrast, Davies' drawing is based upon a representation of Walcot that was far more actualised, since he pointed out that while it 'was partly aspirational, some did happen'.[333] In addition to such infrastructure, the festivals and community-spirited activities of the Bath Arts Workshop made a significant contribution to the area. Davies recalled, for example, that group members used to put on Christmas dinners for up to 200 older people.[334] In this way Bath Arts Workshop members were able to positively create and exploit opportunities outside of the formal economy, making prefigurative spaces where decision-making takes place in workers' cooperatives and surplus can be paid back to the local community, rather than to distant shareholders. Through the Christmas banquets, the hippies were able to bring colour and sociability to Walcot. They helped to break down intergenerational alienation through an act of mutual aid for older Bathonians. Were such community interventions used effectively to build bridges by more radical countercultural groups, such as the Black Panthers, during the previous decade? Or were they a foreshadowing of

331 Angela Carter, 'There's no Such Thing as a Free Lunch: A History of Western Civilisation' (1979), 1, unpublished manuscript in the personal archive of Shirley Cameron and Roland Miller.
332 *Radical Technology*, ed. by Peter Harper, Godfrey Boyle and the editors of *Undercurrents* (London: Wildwood House, 1976), 168-69).
333 Glyn Davies at The Past, Present and Future of Community Energy event, Museum of Bath at Work (15 June 2019).
334 Glyn Davies, personal conversation with the author (Upper Swainswick, 17 July 2016).

Bath Arts Workshop in Walcot.

'big society' voluntarism? These are relevant questions to ask concerning the achievements of the alternative society during the 1970s.

The development of alternative infrastructure and flourishing cultural events in Bath, concentrated in Walcot, described above, were ultimately contained but nevertheless impactful. These localised successes should be considered as a part of a wider appraisal of social well-being during the 1970s. The 1970s was a period that achieved a welfare system that was more supportive and distributive than in subsequent decades, a society in which inequality was decreasing, both in terms of the distribution of economic wealth and due to the ascendance of social movements of anti-racism, women's liberation and gay liberation that were starting to challenge entrenched social inequalities. The collective, integrated social projects established by the Bath Arts Workshop and other groups made for cooperatives and self-employment, a decent quality of life with low capital which was recycled and distributed within the community. More work needs to be done to explore the decision-making and operational structures of such enterprises. The area's counterculture was also enduring. Indeed, expressions of Alternative Walcot have continued to the present day, such as Harvest Wholefoods (constituted as a workers' cooperative) which Carter had affectionately mocked during the 1970s, The Bell (now a community-owned pub) and the regular flea market selling bric-à-brac.

The authentically countercultural aspects of the area as a whole, however, are diminished and diluted. The impressively integrated elements of the Bath Arts Workshop depicted in Davies' drawing have disappeared as a consequence of market forces, changing demographic factors and shifting commitments and priorities. Could it be that such initiatives were viable steps towards a more colourful and emancipated space with scope for participatory democracy and regenerative economic systems at the regional level, and that ground has since been lost? Or were they the forerunners of hipster capitalist entrepreneurship? This a matter for further political assessment. Inevitably, there were also dysfunctional aspects of the counterculture due to ego-clashes, drug and alcohol casualties and profiteering. The district also fell prey to the familiar pattern in which an area's affordability and opportunities, for experimental artists, squatters and the other alternative people that Carter admired and embraced, makes the streets desirable, and hence ripe for encroaching gentrification. Ironically, this ultimately displaces the creative people and energy that made the area an attractive place to live in the first place.

Shirley Cameron, Carter's friend and collaborator during the Bath years and afterwards, reflected upon the different priorities and aspirations of the alternative society that existed at the time:

The counterculture really was quite different. These days people might start out on the margins and they work their way into the mainstream, whatever. In those days that wasn't the ambition; they definitely thought they'd be in the counterculture and they'd stay that way. And, to a certain extent, they've been vindicated. All over the place they started on that journey, in the 1970s there wasn't that ambition really.[335]

Another dimension to Angela Carter's social life and political commitment during her years in Bath was her support for the local Labour Party. She became branch secretary for the Bathwick ward of the Labour Party at a time when her friends Christopher Frayling, Edward Horesh and film director Ken Loach were also active local members. Frayling has fond memories of the cultural front that they established in Century House, a Georgian building that was until recently the Party's premises, where he created an artfully combined montage of radical history and literature mixing inspiration from Soviet realist cinema with classics of the English socialist tradition to Edward Carpenter:

In May 1976—the fiftieth anniversary of the General Strike, which happened from 4-13 May 1976—I put together an audiovisual presentation on the Strike and its legacy for the Bath Labour Party at Century House in Pierrepont Street. Angela was at the time Secretary of the Bathwick ward of the Party (even though it wasn't her ward—it did make the meetings more lively!) and Edward Horesh was the Bath Party's political education officer. I was an ordinary member. There was a taped soundtrack, which involved Angela, Edward and I reading from *The Penguin Book of Socialist Verse*—Thomas Hood, William Morris, Bertolt Brecht—intercut with newspaper accounts of what was happening day by day on the streets.[336]

Unfortunately, as mentioned at the outset, the local Labour Party much reduced its archive when they recently moved premises from the large building in Pierrepont Street into a considerably smaller office in Walcot Street, making it necessary to 'drastically reduce' their paperwork.[337]

335 Shirley Cameron, telephone interview with the author (8 November 2018).
336 Frayling, *Inside the Bloody Chamber*, 38.
337 Mary Flitton (Secretary of Bath Constituency Labour Party), e-mail to the author (15 February 2018).

Comtek: A Tomorrow's World for the Counterculture

Comtek (shorthand for Community Technology) was a major national event, probably the first of its kind, to showcase alternative and community technology. Thornton Kay, Rick Knapp and Glyn Davies founded Comtek which was run as part of a festival in Bath in 1974, 1975 and 1976. Kay records that Comtek attracted as many as 150 national alternative technology and community groups to the city. It had its origins in the Bath Community Design Workshop which started in 1973. It was an offshoot of the Bath Arts Workshop and was a part of the Walcot Festival attended by thousands at this time. The location of the Comtek workshop in Weymouth Street also ensured that Bath was a significant hub for alternative technology throughout the rest of the year.

Architect and artist, Glyn Davies, who moved to Bath in 1972, was involved in Comtek from the start and was photographer for the events. He reminds us that in 1974 not many people had seen the kind of technology on show before and it was still considered very novel.[338] (The Centre for Alternative Technology had only opened the previous year in 1973). Llewellyn suggests that the pioneering spirit of the network of people around Comtek constituted a significant origin for the development and popularisation of the United Kingdom's wind industry.[339] Indeed, even in the present day, the innocent passer-by might still gasp with astonishment, amusement or bewilderment when confronted by some of the more outlandishly experimental paraphernalia that featured in Comtek. In this respect, conspicuous by its central presence was the Belgian group Mass Moving's assembly of a gigantic solar-powered steam trumpet. A concrete-filled car was installed in the former Southgate shopping centre in a bid to liberate the streets from cars for the benefit of pedestrians and cyclists.[340] The programme for *Comtek '74* records that a group called Harsh Mouse unfortunately found their voyage down the River Avon on a huge inflatable sausage was scuppered when their 'craft sprang a leak'.

Sometimes known as the Walcot Sunshine Festival, the illuminating jamboree that was Comtek quickly became a magnet for tinkerers, visionary nowtopians and the plain curious. The creatives who organised the event showcased much that was genuinely innovative to inspire and collaborate. Comtek helped lay the foundations of solar power, wind power and renewable energy for the decades to come. The Comtek circle developed several pieces of technology, such as the Salvonius turbine, the pyramidal stage structure of the

338 Glyn Davies, personal conversation with the author (Upper Swainswick, 17 July 2016).
339 Robert Llewellyn at The Past, Present and Future of Community Energy event, Museum of Bath at Work (15 June 2019).
340 Glyn Davies, personal conversation with the author (Upper Swainswick, 17 July 2016).

AUGUST 2nd to 9th

For the past five years Bath Arts Workshop have been the co-ordinators of a summer festival aimed at providing for the needs of local people. The festivals offer not only entertainment, but also an opportunity for people to get together and help themselves through involvement in the organization and planning of the events.

Bath Arts Workshop see the festivals as an expression of their overall aim to help the individual and the community to become more aware of their own potential.

The "Another Festival" of 1973 was organized by committees of local people, which were set up well in advance, in each of the three main housing areas of the city. Domes were built in each of these areas to enable three community festivals to happen simultaneously with the events in the streets and central venues. During the whole of the 10 -day festival there were about 250 performing artists, over 200 voluntary helpers and a total audience exceeding 30,000.

The festivals were financed partly by holding jumble sales & concerts and partly by grants from the Arts Council of Great Britain, the South Western Arts Association and Bath District Council. However, "with things so expensive" 1974 witnessed the "Last Festival" and the emphasis was on economy. Rather than events taking place allover the city simultaneously, a festival roadshow went around spending three days in each area finishing in Walcot along-side Comtek '74, Britain's first exhibition of community technology. And so it was that the "Last Festival" of community arts came to an end with the introduction of a new concept, -festivals of community technology.

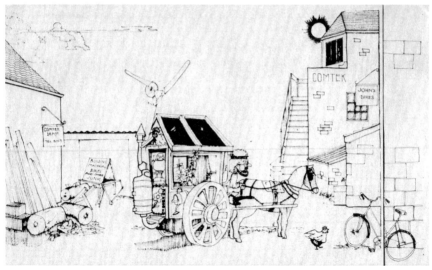

Facing page top left—Programme for the Walcot Sunshine Festival and Comtek (1976).

Facing page bottom—Publicity card for Comtek with its address in Weymouth Street, Walcot, Bath. Drawing by Glyn Davies.

Facing page top right—Newsletter for Walcot Festival and Comtek '75.

This page Top—Community Media van at Comtek '74.

This page bottom—View of Comtek 1975.

kind used at Glastonbury Festival, curvilinear structures made of mesh webs and the Interaction community film-making van, which constituted serious contributions towards socially-orientated technology. The work and ideas of many of those who contributed to Comtek—such as the *Undercurrents* team, Street Farmers and Herbert Girardet—were also to appear within the covers of the main national publication on the subject, *Radical Technology. Radical Technology* praised the *Comtek '74* catalogue which featured a comprehensive directory that included more than 600 addresses for practitioners and suppliers.[341]

The 1975 event, incorporating a Futures Forum, appears to have supported a significantly larger programme. Around 50 groups participated in 1974 which was a four-day gathering. By 1975 Comtek had expanded into a ten-dayer, at which up to 150 alternative technology and community groups exhibited their wares and services. In later years the event relocated to Milton Keynes.

Angela Carter moved from Bath to Clapham in 1976. Unfortunately, some of the 'dishevelled loveliness' that Carter experienced in Bath has been subsequently lost in development blunders such as the huge and controversial dual-carriageway that scars the eastern approaches to the city, and the demolition of the riverside neo-Classical Churchill House to be replaced by bleak, dysfunctional bus station architecture, popularly known as the chip-pan fryer. The class composition of the city remains varied since wealthy owners of complete blocks of Georgian housing live cheek by jowl with tenants renting adjacent blocks that have been divided and sub-divided. Significant pockets of deprivation remain in areas such as Whiteway and Snow Hill since low-incomes are exacerbated by higher than average retail prices. Also, since Angela Carter's day, the booming property market has for the most part priced out the citizens of alternative Bath who fled to the more financially hospitable climes of Bristol, Stroud and Frome.

---

341 Boyle and Harper (eds.), *Radical Technology*, 272.

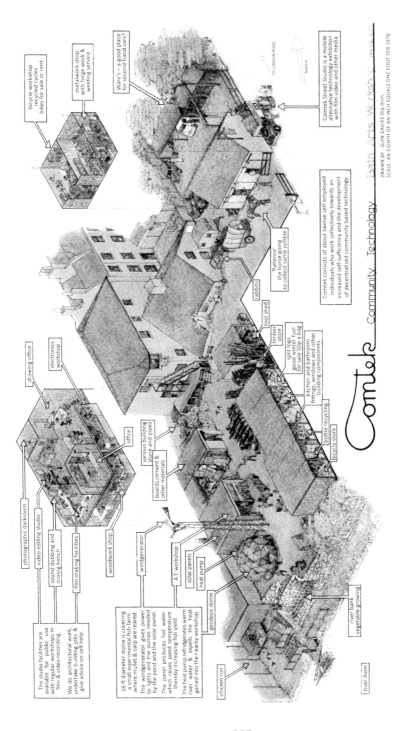

Plan of Bath Arts Workshop's Comtek area (1976), drawn by Glyn Davies.

Final Thoughts on the Somerset of *Love*

The folk music explosion was deeply embedded within the Consciousness Revolution of the 1960s driven by two themes: social and political activism, and the hippy peace and love movement. Some areas of Bristol, such as Clifton, Redland and Cotham, embraced both. In the mid to late 60s, there was a naïve rumour that the seedy 18th/19th century student and artists enclave of Clifton was comparable to Haight Ashbury, in San Francisco. Well… I must state, with reluctance and regret, that Clifton, even with the occasional kimono or spliff, was staid and conservative by comparison. Yet, it was revolutionary with the British consciousness of the day, so that naïve rumour could stand. (Robert Stewart)[342]

Angela Carter spoke of the 'provincial Bohemia' she was familiar with in Bristol during the 1960s. This book has set out to survey that world. Social history is never a clearly structured and coherent account of the past, but rather the residue of events, captured in fragments of memory, any texts that have been kept, images and artefacts from the creative arts and everyday life and, for the last century and a half, audiovisual materials. My sources for the counterculture that contextualises Angela Carter's writings and experiences in Bristol and Bath include a selection of the most relevant of such materials that I have been able to gather together by rambling through the literature and communicating with people who lived in the area at the time. In keeping with the ethos of the Bristol Radical History Group, I have taken a 'history from below' approach, by concerning myself with the unofficial culture of the 1960s and 1970s.

Such a psycho-geographical exploration must, of necessity, be more meandering than linear, pulling together diverse people, places and themes, many with a belief in the need for collective change, but each with their own experiences and priorities. Robert Stewart's observation that Clifton was 'staid and conservative' by comparison with Haight Ashbury is valuable since it is based on first-hand experience, yet something of a truism, given the worldwide reputation of the latter's famous 1967 summer of love. It was, of course, the case that the scale of the 'provincial Bohemia' in Bristol and Bath was much less than, and partly derivative of, the counterculture that was blossoming in larger centres of population. There are some amusing parallels with Haight Ashbury, however, such as Le Mare's memory of tourists visiting late 1950s Hotwells to stare at the spectacle of the beatniks. Sjöö reversed the comparison with American counterparts, writing in a 1968 letter that 'Four of us borrowed

342 Robert Stewart in Jones, *Bristol Folk,* 151.

a car and went to Woodstock, a kind of artists' colony, a sort of Clifton'.[343] More significant is the evidence for an equivalent intensity of experience and variety of alternative ideas and practice present at the 'provincial' level.

Furthermore, the 'enclaves' I have been looking at in Clifton and Bath were far from enclosed but closely networked with alternative initiatives in both metropolitan and rural districts. Poet Spike Hawkins suggested a beautifully dynamic visual image of the relationships that developed:

> London was no more the centre than anywhere else. There was constant movement. We were meeting people, communicating, establishing centres. There was cohesion, as if we had rubber bands stretched all over England and we could just pull one.[344]

Such interconnections were, in fact, global. We have seen, for example, that the Clifton-based artist and anarcha-feminist Monica Sjöö visited social ecologists Murray Bookchin and Bea Bookchin and members of the revolutionary 'Up Against the Wall Motherfuckers' group in the United States. In Bath, such giants of the American counterculture as Jefferson Airplane and Country Joe and the Fish took to the stage, and the city also hosted appearances by the famous beat poet Allen Ginsberg in 1966 and 1973. Moreover, initiatives with their origins in the regional counterculture of the West Country and south Wales, such as Glastonbury Festival (evolving from smaller West Country free festivals) and the women's anti-nuclear protests at Greenham Common (initiated by Welsh activist Ann Pettitt, one-time student occupier at the University of Bristol), were to gain international significance.

Angela Carter's relationship to this counterculture was that of a critical friend. She was a pivotal writer who was enthralled by the 'provincial Bohemia' that she encountered and partially inhabited during the 1960s and 1970s, while at no point losing contact with more mainstream culture. At first sight, it seems her perspective was one of slightly envious detachment:

> She later said that her early years in the city were like living in a museum: there were wonderful things everywhere she looked, but for all she had to do with them, they might as well have been sealed behind glass.[345]

343 White, Monica Sjöö: *Life and Letters*, 41.
344 Spike Hawkins in *Days in the Life: Voices from the English Underground 1961-1971*, ed. by Jonathan Green [first pub. 1988] (London: Pimlico, 1998), 23.
345 Gordon, *Invention of Angela Carter*, 53 (from an unpublished memoir by Carole Howells).

Yet, I would suggest that this sense of alienation was something of a rhetorical stance projected in hindsight, since, as we have seen, she was actively participating in local literary, musical and political social scenes soon after her arrival in Bristol. Accounts of Angela Carter's involvement in the local folk scene differ as to the performance culture that held sway within the clubs that she ran with her husband. They certainly do not, however, suggest disengagement. Living in Clifton's Royal York Crescent during the 1960s, and adjacent to Bath's Walcot during the 1970s, Carter was at the epicentre of the alternative societies that thrived in the West Country in those decades. Some of this persona of separation may be due to her creative need to maintain a distance to be protective of her writer's prerogative to express herself freely, and to better get the measure of the social milieux which were her themes.

As a novelist, Carter was seeking the truth of imaginative writing rather than undertaking reportage. Leading theorist of creativity, Mihaly Csikszentmihalyi, wrote of the relationship between the creative person and his or her output, identifying their creation as 'what we call culture, or those parts of ourselves that we internalized from the social environment'.[346] In Carter's case, she self-realised creatively through her writing by a process of practice and experiment, making use not just of her literary influences but of her social and physical surroundings. She had extraordinary conversations and engaged with the world politically. She was able to identify potential in the raw materials and narrative aspects of her personal situation and to synthesise her experiences through the transformative power of the imagination. She was an inveterate journal keeper, capturing the bricolage of her everyday life, whether a ballad, a street scene or eavesdropping on a conversation in a local pub and using these sources for descriptive colour and sense-making. Carter made use of collage, for example, as a source of inspiration, creating eye-catching collections of labels and cut-outs on her journal covers during the 1960s. Like the characters in *Shadow Dance* and *Love*, she also collected Victorian rubbish. Her alchemical knack for piecing together disparate sources, and, vitally, to transmute them into something fresh and dazzling, was an engaging technique that she would use to ever more consummate effect. In this way, she progressed from the early 'Bristol' novels through to her brilliant final work *Wise Children* (1991), in which a retrospective look back through the scrapbook of the Chance sisters' vaudeville lives is tightly plotted and evoked in seamless continuity.

The immediate draw of person and place is particularly significant in the Bristol trilogy. Attention to the way in which Carter built up closely observed

346 Mihaly Csikszentmihalyi, *Creativity: Flow and the Psychology of Discovery and Invention* (New York: Harper Perennial, 1997), 317.

characterisations, scenarios and anecdotes from her life in Bristol helps to historicise her early realist work. We have seen that the crescents, in their semi-derelict but more affordable condition, attracted many countercultural and creative people to Clifton during the 1960s. In Bath too, some of the dwellings in John Wood's sun-shaped and druidically-inspired Circus were an affordable option, although the accompanying moon of the Royal Crescent remained the preserve of the wealthy. Angela Carter mixed widely, socialising, for example, with musicians and anarchists in Clifton, and alternative performance artists and squatters in Bath. She routinely compiled closely-observed word-sketches and collected characters from the surrounding area, whether street buskers or the clientele of local alehouses, such as The Greyhound, and coffeehouses, such as The Berkeley in Clifton, and recreated them in her fiction. This corroborates O'Day's suggestion that there were important 'circumstantial'[347] as well as literary sources for Carter's early novels, even though she disguised the settings and anonymised the characters.

Such interconnections are best, and most enjoyably, investigated through oral history, direct correspondence and with attention to primary sources. This involves lots of asking around, speaking to people and the fortunes of random chance. All memoirs and oral interviews are based upon the inevitably partial details of incidents and anecdotes that interviewees remembered or chose to recount. An important distinction should also be drawn between the experiencing self, which is conscious of present happenings, and accounts of the remembering self, which selects and reconstructs the details of an occurrence after (in the case of oral history sometimes several decades after) the event.[348] Notwithstanding this caution about retrospective interpretation, direct contact with several people who knew Angela Carter personally and were generous in sharing their memories supplies invaluable first-hand detail that helps to triage the accounts of the critics. As Edmund Gordon concludes in the first full biography of the writer, 'she's much too big for any single book to contain'.[349]

There is some urgency in gathering first-hand accounts of events and experiences that, in the case of the late 1950s, are reaching the limits of living memory. As discussed at the outset, shifting access to documents can also be a factor. It seems you lose some; the Bath Labour Party's documents for the 1970s, the years when Angela Carter was an active participant, are likely to have been

347 O'Day, '"Mutability is Having a Field Day"'.
348 A distinction by Daniel Kahneman who suggests that 'Confusing experience with the memory of it is a compelling cognitive illusion' in *Thinking, Fast and Slow* (London: Allen Lane, 2011), 381.
349 Gordon, *Invention of Angela Carter*, 421.

disposed of recently. But you also win some; the letters of Monica Sjöö have become more accessible since their publication in 2018. These are a valuable source since she was a mostly Bristol-based artist and activist who wholly embraced countercultural perspectives through her lifestyle and work. Taking a psychogeographical approach in loosely navigating through countercultural sources also reveals different themes and raises other questions from previous research. It travels across different territory, for example, from those who have scrutinised Angela Carter's life and work for what it tells us about feminism or for its psychoanalytic approaches. So, what have we learned? And what further questions are raised?

Favourable economic conditions in Bristol and Bath helped to accommodate a viable counterculture during the long 1960s. Among commentators contacted for this research, there has been a consensus that the availability of low-rent housing, and in some cases opportunities for squatting, attracted a critical mass of creative workers and people with alternative perspectives. The high levels of employment also freed up space for experimentation at this time. There is a perception that those who dropped out during the comparatively affluent 1960s could usually find paid work for a particular project or adventure when times were hard.[350] These over-arching circumstances help to explain the cities' flourishing alternative society. But they also account for its demise during times of economic downturn. Unemployment remained low throughout the 1950s and 1960s, before steadily rising during the 1970s and escalating considerably during the Thatcher years. In the case of Bristol and Bath, the favourable situation regarding affordable rent began to change during the mid-1970s. Consequently, people involved in the counterculture increasingly relocated as they were priced out of accommodation in areas such as Clifton and Walcot. In response, community activist groups such as the Clifton Tenants' Association formed to resist poor housing conditions and evictions. Both Clifton and Walcot demonstrate the familiar pattern of gentrification. Both were attractive to people involved in experimenting in alternatives, due to their relative affordability, well-connected locations, appealing historic architecture and green spaces and diverse populations. The creative changes this critical mass of people brought about turned such areas into desirable destinations and therefore subject to significant price inflation, eventually resulting in the exodus of those that had added cultural value.

The systemic increases in social inequality dating from the Thatcher era,

---

350 See, for instance, comments of Peter Roberts in Green (ed.) *Days in the Life: Voices from the English Underground 1961-1971,* 49. Sandbrook confirms there was consistently low unemployment during the 1960s, with a modest increase in 1967 in *White Heat*, 88, 305, 416, 785.

and the squeeze on living conditions due to mass unemployment during the 1980s and austerity, especially since 2008, have made it increasingly difficult for non-market alternatives to exist within capitalist society. Debates continue as to the extent to which aspects of the counterculture, characterised by lifestylism and individualism, made its recuperation inevitable, by facilitating a market-driven entrepreneurial culture.[351] Potentially viable, sustainable alternatives grounded in ideas such as those put forward by Murray Bookchin or E. F. Schumacher during the 1960s and 1970s have not been adopted or implemented. The revolutionary aspects of the counterculture based on resistance to recuperation and taking uncompromising positions existed in the gaps and margins of mainstream culture. Such a predicament often left such groups fragmented, economically weak and socially disempowered so rarely able to defend themselves against the onslaught of state and capital. Stuart Christie, a prominent anarchist who spent time in Bristol during the 1960s, became disillusioned by what he regarded as the shortcomings and limited aspirations of parts of the counterculture as its exponents accommodated themselves to comfortable hedonism and lost their hunger for radical change:

> The counter-culture was becoming an end in itself rather than a means to an end. On the whole they were a creative, colourful and cheery lot whose hearts were in the right place, but no way was racism going to be eliminated or the steadily escalating Vietnam War stopped by good vibrations alone.[352]

The measure of this reduced effectiveness in mobilising potential resistance came in the wake of the prominent defeat of organised labour in the form of the miners' communities and print workers and dissident minorities such as travellers, ravers and disaffected youth in the once explosive inner-cities. Interstitial activism and lifestyle countercultures could generate alternative micro-communities but at that time ultimately lacked the means to bring about the wider solidarity necessary to achieve meaningful change, build up supportive infrastructure or extensively take over the means of production. Without such democratic control, it is difficult to prioritise a decent material standard of living, health and education for all of society on the socialist model, over the inequities and inefficiencies of consumer capitalism. That said, the promise of imaginative means to take workers' control of industry, in part

---

351 It became clear in the mid-1960s that the underground represented a great potential market to exploit and that this could be a problem. See for example Chris Rowley's comments in Green (ed.) *Days in the Life: Voices from the English Underground 1961-1971*, 175.
352 Christie, *Granny Made Me An Anarchist* (London: Simon & Schuster, 2005), 260.

derived from syndicalist ideas, were perhaps more widespread and progressive than in the present day, when advocates of authentic change are demoralised due to more factors than it is possible to explore here. Angela Carter saw the dangers of Thatcherism of which she was sharply critical during the 1980s and up to the end of her life in 1992.

There have been several references to beatniks, who appeared at the beginning of the period of research, from the late 1950s onwards. There is scope for more work on the character and impact of the beatnik movement in the West Country. This was reflected in the influence of American Beat poetry and the presence of a small beat culture with a cluster of venues where beatniks would receive a sympathetic welcome. Peter Le Mare remembered from personal experience that The Three Tuns in Hotwells, for instance, was a known beatnik hangout, while Ian A. Anderson numbered beatniks among the customers of Clifton's Troubadour Club, established in 1966. Linked to the jazz scene, many of the beatniks also become politically and culturally involved with CND. Beatniks were attracted to the wider West Country, with Devon's so-called English Riviera and St Ives and other parts of south Cornwall being particularly favoured spots. It seems that the beatniks were met with a mixture of bemusement and hostility in the press and some sections of the local population, but further revelations concerning west-country expressions of this sub-culture would be welcome.

One concern that has come out of personal recollections has been the wish to offer a corrective to negative characterisations of Paul Carter. Commentators who had been friends with both Angela and Paul Carter in Bristol during the 1960s were keen to redress what they regarded as the negative impression of the latter in recent accounts. Christine Molan felt that Gordon's biography, *The Invention of Angela Carter* was 'shamefully loaded' against Paul, who declined to be interviewed for the book when he was also nearing the end of his life, and that the editing of the material collated for the BBC *Of Wolves and Women* documentary resulted in a 'negative emphasis [that] gave a very distorted view of [Angela's] Bristol folk activities and (again) Paul, who taught her (as she said) everything about folk music'.[353] Neil Curry wrote of Paul's supportive role during their marriage, commenting that 'Living with [Angela] cannot have been easy! Recent TV programme [*Of Wolves and Women*] denigrated him. He was very likeable. We all liked him'.[354] Bob Gale, who initially knew both Paul and Angela through the early 1960s folk clubs, also disapproved of the documentary because 'It was down on Paul Carter, giving the impression

353 Christine Molan, e-mails to the author (25 October 2018 and 26 November 2018).
354 Neil Curry, e-mail to the author (3 October 2018).

that he was holding [Angela] back, which was completely untrue'.[355] Such accounts therefore reveal and put on the record that recent representations of Paul Carter are contested.

If it is true that there was a thoroughgoing cultural transformation during the 1960s and 1970s, the idea that the personal was political gained currency and was central to this shift. The relationship between Angela and Paul Carter perhaps tracked the shift away from the lifelong monogamy expected of 1950s middle-class couples in nuclear relationships. The breakdown in their marriage at the end of their decade in Bristol suggests that Angela felt that a divorce was necessary to her future self-growth and positive life experience. Carter's outlook was countercultural, later becoming a prominent critic of Thatcherism, yet it would perhaps be more accurate to describe her as contrarian rather than a full-blown revolutionary. As we have seen, in 1972 she called herself 'in a slap-dash kind of way, an anarcho-Marxist',[356] a self-description that is characteristically fluid. In this way she allows herself to retain room for political manoeuvre in the very act of affirming and asserting a stance, one in part influenced by discussions with Bristol anarchists. When she was involved with the Labour Party in Bath it was to be from the libertarian socialist wing of the party, supporting internationalism and workers' control of industry rather than nationalism and nationalisation. If the precise terms of her commitment were uncertain, Carter's ongoing engagement was never in doubt.[357]

The small Bristol anarchist scene was linked to interventions in alternative theatre, a form of politics by other means that always appealed to Carter. I have touched upon the controversy of the Carters' reputation for rather exclusive purism and that Angela Carter was remembered, bluntly, in fellow student Peter Bild's words, as 'singing in an aggressively "finger-in-the-ear" manner' that wasn't everyone's taste'.[358] It seems, however, that the Carters were involved in other activities at the Lansdown that, so far as I am aware, have previously been unrecorded. These suggest a different story, one that sounds like something from within the realms of one of Carter's own fantastical tales. Her involvement in the alternative happenings of the Grot Club, including the spoof religion of 'Mojoism', is an unexplored and unexpected aspect of her activities in 1960s Clifton. I have speculated that this was connected to Carter's curiosity about Alfred Jarry's work and ideas about 'pataphysics which were in vogue in some countercultural circles at the time. Barry

355 Bob Gale, telephone interview with the author (26 November 2018).
356 Letter to Marion Boyars received 9 October 1972, quoted in Anna Watz, Angela Carter and Surrealism: 'A Feminist Libertarian Aesthetic' (London: Routledge, 2017), 1.
357 Asked in an interview if her political allegiances were the same as when she was 18 years old, Carter responded 'Yes—sceptical Left.' 'Back Page', *Marxism Today* (July 1991), 48.
358 Peter Bild, e-mail to the author (29 December 2018).

Flanagan, for example, who lived in neighbouring Cornwallis Crescent and shared mutual friends in Nick Gray and Corinna Sargood, enthusiastically embraced 'pataphysics. The Grot Club and Mojoism seem to both celebrate the creativity of the 1960s but also mock some of the darker, cultish aspects of the era. Certainly, active participation in dramatic performances formed part of Carter's experiences in Bath in the 1970s. It would be interesting to find out more about her involvement in theatrical experimentation in Bristol, and the extent to which she was a spectator or active participant.

Experimentation with psychedelic drugs was also popular with sections of the 1960s and 1970s counterculture. Apart from the possibly mind-altering properties of West Country scrumpy,[359] however, there is no evidence that Carter's hallucinatory writing can be attributed to the psychedelic drug scene that had developed within the West Country's counterculture by the late 1960s. Although the absence of evidence is not evidence of absence, there is no suggestion that LSD's imaginative properties inspired her creative work.

The counterculture in London and the West Country bears comparison, but there are also contrasts. We have seen that personal networking strengthened the relationship between the provincial bohemia to be found in Bristol and Bath and the extensive counterculture in London and internationally. As we would expect, concerns about nuclear war, the Vietnam War and the 1968 uprisings in Paris were expressed in local demonstrations. A small number of squats appeared in Bristol, but unlike the capital, no squatter communities were established. More prominently, mobilisations such as the Bristol Bus Boycott in the 1960s, around women's liberation and festival culture in the 1970s, and against nuclear weapons in the 1980s, all showed the West Country to be a progressive region. A critical mass of people participating, or aspiring to, alternative lifestyles in districts such as Clifton and Walcot found their expression in collective activism, creative output, and the kind of informal or coordinated events that contributed to the festal atmosphere that Angela Carter later remembered fondly.

Alongside the provincial bohemia's outward-looking aspects, the circumscribed geographical areas of Clifton and Walcot made for a neighbourhood intimacy that brought about valuable face-to-face communication too. In the case of the Bath Arts Workshop, for example, physical proximity drew people together enabling them to coordinate events which gained national prominence, such as the Bath Festival of the Blues, in 1969, and the Comtek festivals of alternative technology, in the mid-1970s.

359 The landlord of Carter's Bath local, The Bell in Walcot Street, claimed of his draft cider that 'you can actually feel [it] making contact with your central nervous system' according to Frayling, *Inside the Bloody Chamber*, 18).

This informal and organic concentration of agitators, dreamers and doers can bring about creative happenstance, to produce—in an over-used term—synergies. Film director Spike Lee recently spoke of the value of creative neighbourhoods, such as the one he thrived in the 1980s in Brooklyn, to facilitate artistic expression and movements. Lee celebrated the advantages and opportunities of the kind of personal contact lacking in online, virtual communities, asserting that 'It's gotta be face-to-face. We were all bumping into each other on the block here'.[360] Provincial bohemia also seems to have been more inclusive than metropolitan varieties, with the kind of cultural elitism that critics alleged was endemic in the underground scene in London,[361] being less evident in the West Country. Further perspectives would need to be sought to verify whether this was the case.

The 1960s counterculture faced threats from within as well as without. It is a loose overarching term that includes multiple worldviews and even contradictory principles. Some of these are represented among the provincial bohemians who appear in Carter's Bristol trilogy. She was fascinated by the society she encountered when she moved to the West Country. Her works from this era present a multidimensional set of characters and situations and reveal facets of the counterculture they represent through all their foibles, cruelties, guile and gusto. It is not her role as a novelist to celebrate, endorse or condemn them. Egotistical hedonism could slip into outright dysfunctional and anti-social elements of the counterculture. The sadistic persona of Honeybuzzard is the most prominent example of such a trait, indulging in exploitation and violent abuse in *Shadow Dance*. Honeybuzzard's faux charisma is a cover for acts of self-aggrandisement and self-gratification. Positively, there are characters of the festal late 1960s that attempt to achieve self-realisation by finding moments of collective enchantment and experimenting creatively, who carry out small acts of liberation and altruistic kindnesses and demonstrate empathy and connection. Joseph Harker, the anti-hero and morgue worker in *Several Perceptions*, transcends his depression and condition of alienation as the novel unfolds, leading to a more joyous, though ultimately provisional and equivocal, ending. As suggested, the counterculture also included elements of individualism, hedonism and commercialism that rendered its creative output vulnerable to appropriation by the mainstream during the succeeding, more conservative, decades.

360 Tim Adams, 'Interview: Spike Lee', *The Guardian* (29 July 2018): https://www.theguardian.com/film/2018/jul/29/spike-lee-interview-blackkklansmen-film [accessed 11 December 2018].

361 A complaint common to several commentators in Green (ed.) *Days in the Life: Voices from the English Underground 1961-1971*, 187-189 and 211.

'Wild Bristol' image from *Bristol Voice* (May 1978).

In 1987 Carter wrote an afterword to the 1969 novel *Love*, imagining the fates of her characters nearly two decades later. Here the novelist suggests that some apparently countercultural mindsets were fully compatible with the social and political trends that followed, facilitating rather than in conflict with them. The major character Buzz, we are told, becomes a club manager and 'dabbled in real estate'. The 'peroxided psychiatrist' becomes the director of three pharmaceutical companies, the author of *How to Succeed Even Though You Are a Woman* and 'drives a Porsche, rather fast'. Carolyn becomes a wealthy television presenter, marries a barrister and joins the Social Democratic Party.[362] Such characters seamlessly undertook the journey from hippiedom to yuppiedom as the Thatcher years advanced.

So, what happened to the counterculture of the 1960s and 1970s? Did it scale up into mainstream culture, shrink, dissipate, mutate or evolve? As we have seen, the counterculture was a diverse thing a case could be made that each of these happened.

Angela Carter's final words in the semi-realist Bristol trilogy, therefore, conclude with some of her characters' personal outcomes from the shifting environment in which they find themselves. The novels are political in as much as they deal with social and historic spaces which capitalism tends to privatise, colonise and obliterate. The 1960s followed a recent period of the most cataclysmic warfare the world had ever experienced in the early 1940s, austerity in the late 1940s and escalating consumerism in the 1950s (which was already proving to be problematic). By the end of the decade diverse countercultural trends—from enthusiasm for inner change through spiritual transformation, psychedelic exploration or anti-psychiatry to the multiple

362 Carter, Afterword to *Love*, 113-120.

forms of political engagement undertaken by the New Left—had emerged in ways that were both mutually informing and fractious. It is a big ask of community initiatives to not only thrive and survive but to develop from a counterculture to a counter-economy, able to replace the dominance of the capitalism on stilts that emerged as the full-blown New Right at the end of the 1970s. It was only in rare historical moments, such as May 1968, when labour organisations and social dissidents in the youth movement and beyond united in resistance, that an integrated challenge to state and capital appeared possible. The cultural theorists of the 1980s, in their analysis of the hippies, challenged the effectiveness and authenticity of countercultural initiatives in early drafts, written a decade or two after the phenomenon they were describing. Angela McRobbie, for example, referred to 'an extensive semi-entrepreneurial network which became known as the counter-culture'.[363] This was prescient in revealing the contradictions in building efforts for social transformation around market-oriented practices, however, 'alternative' they may purport to be. While the 1960s were still in full swing, Carter was quick to explore the implications of current efforts towards of self-curation and performance in her essay 'Towards a Sixties Style' (1967). As alternative culture became more mainstream there was an impetus to balance the tension between individual identity and collective solidarity. The counterculture's challenge, during the 1960s and 1970s and in the present day, has been to integrate the desire for individual and local autonomy with the recognition that personal self-realization can only be achieved in the struggle for wider social transformation and respect for the community of beings at the international and planetary level. To date, the counterculture has not successfully foregrounded this challenge to act local, think global.

For all the undoubted cultural shifts that the 1960s represented, there were significant limits to the political change that had occurred by 1970, the year that Edward Heath's Conservative government came to power. In a sense the counterculture only emerged due to dissatisfaction with the conservativism of mainstream culture, which remained entrenched. One of the Bristol interviewees, Bob Baker, acknowledged the underlying continuity and the limits to change:

> I had long hair, and the obligatory moustache, but I wasn't really a hippy. I loved the audacity of the rock stars that were bred in the '60s or came out of the '60s and that's the way I felt free. Of course,

363 Angela McRobbie, 'Second-Hand Dresses and the Role of the Ragmarket', 23-49 in *Zoot Suits and Second-Hand Dresses: An Anthology of Fashion and Music*, ed. by Angela McRobbie (Basingstoke: Macmillan, 1989), 34-35.

we weren't free! I mean the Establishment was exactly the same, but they allowed us to have long hair and to wear silly clothes and things, wearing guards' uniforms.[364]

Critics within the counterculture, such as Murray Bookchin, attacked the emphasis upon personal lifestyle change within swathes of the alternative society. Bookchin believed such individualism was ultimately an expression of the division and alienation that stood in the way of collective action for the more profound social transformation in political and economic structures that was necessary to confront the current unsustainable capitalist system and replace it with a more rational alternative.[365]

Bookchin's scepticism and fears have largely been borne out by events. The 1960s counterculture unquestionably had a major cultural effect, for example in its impact on style in rock, fashion and design, or even as in part a source of the internet. In such cases, it becomes a part of the fabric and infrastructure of the mainstream. However, if it were ever its aim, the counterculture failed to bring about the replacement of capitalism with a society based on direct democracy and a sustainable, radically distributive economy. The counter-economy, confined to gaps and surpluses within capitalism, was vulnerable to attack during times of austerity, and left the commanding heights of the economy unchallenged. The failure is also largely explained by the fact that, as we have seen, the idea of a singular counterculture is a misnomer, since it included (and includes) a variety of constituencies that united only in rare and temporary circumstances. When such occasions occurred, as arguably in May 1968, the collective challenge of the New Left to the establishment (itself never as monolithic as this term suggests) was probably greater than at any moment in recent history. Subsequent outbreaks of unity, such as resistance to the poll tax and the Iraq war (the former was undoubtedly more wide-ranging and impactful than the latter), were largely concerned with single issues. It is telling that the most politically radical of the succeeding punk movement were those most fully immersed in the countercultural ideas of the late 1960s, namely anarcho-punk bands such as Crass, The Poison Girls and Chumbawumba. Just as there was no single counterculture there can be no simple conclusion. The counterculture had some modest successes and was important in its own right; many of that generation considering that, for all its weaknesses, absurdities and cruelties, it was the most hopeful and exhilarating time of their lives. On the other hand, aspects of the counterculture were

364 Bob Baker, Skype interview with the author (24 January 2019).
365 Murray Bookchin, *Social Anarchism or Lifestyle Anarchism: An Unbridgeable Chasm* (Edinburgh: AK Press, 1995).

Top—Royal York Crescent, January 1962. This photograph was taken shortly after the Carters moved into number 38.

Bottom—Advertisement for 'Focus', an indoor craft market in Clifton, *Bristol Voice* (1977).

Bristol's long-running Full Marks Bookshop was a favourite outlet for left-wing literature and ideas from the 1970s onwards.

either already predecessors of neo-liberal enterprise or were to be readily recuperated. The counterculture failed to articulate, integrate and bring about a social revolution.

Another conclusion is that the counterculture still exists. Angela Carter enjoyed the emancipatory non-conformism that appeared to be rising across the planet from Paris to Tokyo to Mexico City to smaller places such as her own Bristol, during the 1960s and 1970s. She was intrigued and excited by the possibilities for change, even if she tempered this regard with her customary bemusement and scepticism. She explored, mocked, criticised and celebrated the provincial bohemia around her and the wider counterculture of the times. Since her passing, new countercultural movements have arisen and dissipated, such as Reclaim The Streets and the Occupy Movement. Currently, Extinction Rebellion, Earth Strike and Green Anti-Capitalist Front are gaining media interest, and on the ascendant, searching for fresh strategies for change. To make an effective breakthrough they will need to recognise the importance of class to ecological matters and the necessity to green class politics. The need to make meaningful and sustained interventions in the face of the fake anti-elitism of so-called right-wing populism—promoting the interests of big money and all too often blaming and attacking the most economically vulnerable—is more urgent than ever. In this context, it is important to revisit the 1960s utopian counterculture which dared to experiment and to explore the possibilities for thoroughgoing social change, workers' control, social justice and equality, participatory democracy, liberation and ecological sustainability and to grapple with the tensions between them all. In a sense, there can be no such thing as a failed utopia, only failed aspirations. 'Utopia', a perfectly realised society, would logically transcend imperfections. Such a destination sounds too much like heaven, a supernatural 'no place'. But the more modest objective for radical human progress is one that not only makes social life meaningful but is essential if the fool's paradise of capitalism is to be toppled before it unleashes even more poverty, alienation and ill-being at the individual level, and conflict and environmental devastation at the global level.

To ask whether the counterculture changed the world, therefore, is not to pose the most useful question. It is impossible not to change the world; it is the ability to change the paradigm that is significant and at stake. And, so, some final words to Angela Carter, whose comments on engaging with a text in a 1985 interview in *Marxism Today* could equally well be applied to her fictional encounters with the real counterculture that she knew in Bristol and Bath. Here, she argues that reading cultural and historic artefacts are conversations between self and other that call for powerful personal engagement:

> Reading a book is like re-writing it for yourself. And I think that all fiction is open-ended. You bring to a novel, anything you read, all your experience of the world. You bring your history and you understand it in your own terms.[366]

'Wild Bristol' image from *Bristol Voice* (May 1978).

366 Interview with Angela Carter, 'The Company of Angela Carter: An Interview', *Marxism Today* (January 1985), 20.

Waiter, waiter,
There's a tartan tortoise in my soup!
Yes, madame,
*It's McTurtle soup!**

*No reptiles were harmed in the reprinting
of this Angela Carter joke.

(Courtesy of Neil Curry).

Picture Credits

Front cover: Angela Carter by Fay Godwin © British Library Board, reproduced with permission: https://www.bl.uk/people/angela-carter

Page 3: Ground Floor Flat, 38 Royal York Crescent (Stephen Hunt, 23 June 2018).

Page 13: 'Booming Bristol', from *Evening Post* (10 March 1967). Credit: Bristol Post.

Page 15: Covers of *Songs from Aldermaston*,1960 (from author's archive).

Page 17: Campaign for Nuclear Disarmament march, Broadmead, early 1960s. Bristol Archives, Pol/Ph/5/2. Records of Bristol Constabulary (1836-1974) and Avon & Somerset Constabulary (1974-)–1836-2009.

Page 18: 'This is best Aldermaston yet, says Canon Collins', *Evening Post*, p. 12 (21 April 1962). Credit: Bristol Post.

Page 18: 'And Anna Went Barefoot…', *Western Daily Press and Mirror*, p. 1 (16 May 1960). Credit: Bristol Post.

Page 21: Vietnam marchers in Bristol city centre, *Evening Post* (31 May 1968). Credit: Bristol Post.

Page 21: Advertisement for the Vietnam Folk Concert in Bristol, *Evening Post* (30 May 1968). Credit: Bristol Post.

Page 24: *Greenham News Letter* (January 1995). University of Bristol Special Collections Archive: Pat V T West Papers: DM2123/1/Archive Box 92 File 2 Cuttings.

Page 27: Covers of Topic Record releases, with sleeve notes by Angela Carter.

Page 30: Listing for the Folksong and Ballad club (1964) *English Folk Dance and Song Society: Bristol District* (Autumn 1964), p.5. Bristol Reference Library B 23306: RLPr2Pb Societies II.

Page 35: Ian Vine and Peter Bild from: 'I've no Evidence says Police Chief', *Evening Post* (15 March 1965), p.1. Credit: Bristol Post.

Page 37: Folk graphic from *Bristol Voice* (August 1976), p.14.

Page 39: The Who at Colston Hall, 24 June 1964. Credit: Bristol Post.

Page 39: Bowling at the New Bristol Centre, 12 February 1967. Credit: Bristol Post.

Page 57: Clifton's Royal York Crescent (1962). Photo credit: Brizzle Born and Bred Flickr. Due diligence search for copyright owner undertaken.

Page 62: The Bristol Troubadour gang, Royal York Crescent, 1970. Photograph kindly supplied by Ian A. Anderson.

Page 63: Bristol Visual and Environmental Group, 'Plant a Tree in '73', *Environmental News* (1973). Bristol Reference Library A2 pb Periodicals miscellaneous B25911.

Page 65: Sleeve cover for Ian A. Anderson's *Royal York Crescent* (1970).

Page 67: 32 West Mall, Clifton (Stephen Hunt, 26 December 2018).

Page 70: Annabel Rees (née Lawson), Jeremy Rees, and John Orsborn at the opening of the Arnolfini, March 1961. Reproduced with permission, courtesy of Arnolfini and Bristol Archives'.

Page 71: Clenched fist fretboard image from *Bristol Voice* (August 1976), p.14.

Page 74: Cover of Nick Wayte's poetry collection, *Seconds* (1969).

Page 85: Workers Hold Mass Meeting' (p. 1), Woman in a Man's World' (p. 10) and Bristol Engineers on March to Brandon Hill' (p. 10) *Evening Post* (15 March 1968). Credit: Bristol Post.

Page 88: The Berkeley café in Bristol's Queens Road. Credit: Bristol Post.

Page 94: 'Students holding banners hide their faces as they demonstrate in front of Senate House today', *Evening Post* (9 December 1968). Credit: Bristol Post.

Page 94: 'Support Grows as Senate Sit-In Continues', Special Sit-in Supplement, *Nonesuch News* (7 December 1968). University of Bristol Special Collections: Student Occupations DM 1635/ Box 2 Sit-in 1968.

Page 95: Complicity statement from University of Bristol Special Collections: Student Occupations DM 1635/ Box 2 Sit-in 1968.

Page 95: 'It keeps them off the streets': cartoon from *Nonesuch News* (28 February 1969), 3. University of Bristol Special Collections: Student Occupations DM 1635/ Box 2 Sit-in 1968.

Page 98: Jeremy Brien, 'Paris Fury: Now City of Devastation… And in Bristol Today 100 on March', *Evening Post* (25 May 1968), p.1. Credit: Bristol Post.

Page 100: Election publicity leaflet for Dave Hayles of the Bristol Dwarf Party (1971), kindly supplied by Rod Goodway.

Page 102: Bristol Dwarf Party flier (1971), kindly provided by Rod Goodway.

Page 104: ukrockfestivals.com homepage, 'The Bristol Free Festival 1971', photograph of Bristol Dwarfs by Gordon Strong (reproduced with permission): http://www.ukrockfestivals.com/bristol-free-festival-1971.html [accessed 18 January 2019].

Page 107: Front cover of *Seeds* 3: *Bristol's Street Press* [1971]. (From author's archive).

Page 109: Front cover of *SPAM* no. 2 [1972]. Bristol Reference Library: RL Pr 2 Pb Newspapers II B 25908.

Page 110: 'It's a great area…so uplifting!!', *SPAM* no.2 [1972]. Bristol Reference Library RL Pr 2 Pb Newspapers II B 25908.

Page 110: 'I understand he's from the Planning Department', *SPAM*, no .9 [1974], p.7. Bristol Reference Library RL Pr 2 Pb Newspapers II B 25908.

Page 110: 'Who Rules Bristol?' *Tenants' News*, Special no, 6 (April 1974), p.1. Bristol Reference Library PR 2 pb Periodicals miscellaneous II B26502.

Page 113: 'Architects' Summer Tour: "Wow! That must be more than 30 million square feet of office space out there!",' *Tenants' News* Special no, 6 (April 1974), p.11. Bristol Reference Library PR 2 pb Periodicals miscellaneous II B26502.

Page 113: 'Well they wanted some housing as well', *Tenants' News* Special no, 5 (March 1974), p.5. Bristol Reference Library PR 2 pb Periodicals miscellaneous II B26502.

Page 117: 'Wild Tree-Woman' by Beverly Skinner from *To Be or Not to Be* (Clifton, Bristol: self-published by Beverly Skinner, 1978). Document in author's archive, believed to be extract from 'The Book of Paradise on Earth'. Due diligence search for copyright owner undertaken.

Page 117: Beverly Skinner, *A dove near a fig tree, Bristol, england, 1969*'; Photograph of Beverly Skinner (c1970), captioned: 'Making the Paradise on Earth is the best solution, for mortals and immortals'; Beverly Skinner, 'A Sunday Afternoon Walk, in Bristol at Ashton Court Park: A SELF-PORTAIT OF THE ARTIST & HER SON: CAMERON; AND A FRIEND & HIS DOG' (1968). All three images from University of Bristol Special Collections Archive: Pat V T West Papers: DM2123/1/Archive Box 92 File 2 (Beverly Skinner). Due diligence search for copyright owner undertaken.

Page 118: Early issues of *Enough: The Journal of the Bristol Women's Liberation Group.* Supplied by the Feminist Archive South, Trinity Road Library, Bristol in 2004.

Page 118: Front cover of Monica Sjöö, Liz Moore and Ann Berg, *Towards a Revolutionary Feminist Art* (Bristol: self-published by Monica Sjöö, [1972]). This document is available online from the National Library of Australia: http://nla.gov.au/nla.obj-51715850/view?partId=nla.obj-51715869 [accessed 20 February 2019].

Page 121: Hay Hill, Bath, where Angela Carter lived from 1973-1976 (Stephen Hunt, 23 June 2018).

Page 122: Ticket for anarchist poetry performance organised in Bath by Dennis Gould and Pat VT West in 1965. Kindly supplied to the author by Dennis Gould.

Page 127: Shirley Cameron and Roland Miller, 'Insides', Walcot Village Hall, Bath (1974). Photograph by Roger Perry. From the personal archive of Shirley Cameron and Roland Miller (reproduced with kind permission).

Page 127: Exhibition artwork by Roland Miller and Shirley Cameron (drawn in 1975). From the personal archive of Shirley Cameron and Roland Miller (reproduced with kind permission).

Page 127: Shirley Cameron and Roland Miller, 'Spotted Window', Bath Arts Workshop shop, Walcot Street, Bath (1975). From the personal archive of Shirley Cameron and Roland Miller (reproduced with kind permission).

Page 128: The head of a beast used in *Ceremonies and Transformations of the Beasts*, a production by Shirley Cameron, Roland Miller, Angela Carter (the scriptwriter) and Miguel Yeco in Walcot Village Hall, Bath (1977). From the personal collection of Shirley Cameron and Roland Miller (reproduced with kind permission (photograph by Stephen Hunt, 25 January 2019).

Page 130: Bath Arts Workshop, 1970s (Photograph, Glyn Davies). Kindly supplied by Glyn Davies.

Page 134: Programme for the Walcot Sunshine Festival and Comtek (1976). From the personal archive of Shirley Cameron and Roland Miller, Sheffield. Kindly supplied by Shirley Cameron.

Page 134: Newsletter for Walcot Festival and Comtek '75. Kindly supplied by Glyn Davies.

Page 134: Publicity card for Comtek, with its address at Weymouth Street, Walcot, Bath. Drawing by Glyn Davis. Kindly supplied by Glyn Davies.

Index